O NOBLE HEART

O EDEL HERZ

FRAKTUR AND SPIRITUALITY IN
PENNSYLVANIA GERMAN FOLK ART

THE
HERITAGE
CENTER
MUSEUM
OF
LANCASTER
COUNTY

THE
DONNING COMPANY
PUBLISHERS

Figure 43: Conrad Gilbert. Presentation *fraktur* for Anna Maria Gerhard, 1787. The schoolteacher/*fraktur* artist Conrad Gilbert made many small drawings and texts in the form of presentation frakturs for his pupils. Unlike Isaac Hunsicker's large text (fig. 39) made for wall display, Gilbert's pieces are small and most likely found their way into pupils' schoolbooks. (Courtesy of the National Gallery of Art, gift of Edgar William and Bernice Garbisch Chrysler, No. NGA B-25, 135)

O NOBLE HEART
O EDEL HERZ

FRAKTUR AND SPIRITUALITY IN PENNSYLVANIA GERMAN FOLK ART

BY MICHAEL S. BIRD

Copyright © 2002 by The Heritage Center Museum

All rights reserved, including the right to reproduce this work in any form whatsoever without permission in writing from the publisher, except for brief passages in connection with a review. For information, write:
The Donning Company/Publishers
184 Business Park Drive, Suite 206
Virginia Beach, VA 23462

Steve Mull, General Manager
Mary Taylor, Project Director
Susan Adams, Project Research Coordinator
Barbara B. Buchanan, Office Manager
Richard A. Horwege, Senior Editor
Lori Wiley, Designer
Scott Rule, Senior Marketing Coordinator
Travis Gallop, Marketing Assistant

Library of Congress Cataloging-in-Publication Data

Bird, Michael S., 1941–
　　　O Noble Heart/O Edel Herz : fraktur and spirituality in Pennsylvania German folk art / by Michael S. Bird.
　　　　　　p. cm.
　　　Includes bibliographical references and index.
　　　ISBN 1-57864-166-7 (softcover : alk. paper)
　　　1. Fraktur art—Pennsylvania—Pennsylvania Dutch Country. 2. Pennsylvania Dutch—Religion. 3. Protestant churches—Pennsylvania—Pennsylvania Dutch Country. I. Title.

ND3035.P42 B57 2002
745.6'7089310748—dc21   2002022453
Printed in the United States of America

CONTENTS

ACKNOWLEDGMENTS / 6
PREFACE / 7

INTRODUCTION / 9
RELIGION, ART, AND PENNSYLVANIA GERMAN FRAKTUR

CHAPTER I / 23
CONTEXTS: TAUFSCHEIN, VORSCHRIFT, AND OTHER TEXTS

CHAPTER II / 53
THE WIDE SWEEP OF PIETISM: PENNSYLVANIA GERMAN RELIGION WITHOUT BORDERS

CHAPTER III / 63
REPRESENTATIONAL ART: PICTORIAL IMAGERY IN FRAKTUR

CHAPTER IV / 85
BEHOLD THE MAN: THE MANY CHARACTERIZATIONS OF JESUS

CHAPTER V / 101
LIFE'S JOURNEYS: STAGES, PATHS, MAZES, AND LABYRINTHS

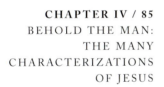

CHAPTER VI / 115
MEMENTO MORI/TEMPUS FUGIT: MORTALITY AND TIME IN FRAKTUR TEXTS

CHAPTER VII / 129
AND THE ANGELS SING: MUSIC AND FRAKTUR

CHAPTER VIII / 139
SYMBOL BY DESIGN: INTENTIONAL CORRELATIONS OF TEXT AND IMAGE

CONCLUSION / 145
THAT WHICH GROWS GREEN TO THE HONOR OF GOD

BIBLIOGRAPHY / 151

INDEX / 156

ABOUT THE AUTHOR / 160

ACKNOWLEDGMENTS

Many are those whose support have made possible the present undertaking. Some are curators, archivists, and directors of institutions, others are scholars in the area of Pennsylvania German material culture, and still others are knowledgeable collectors who have permitted the study and inclusion of *fraktur* in their collections. In the museum field, Peter Seibert, director of the Heritage Center Museum of Lancaster County has been endlessly supportive and enthusiastic in the undertaking of the current publication and related *fraktur* exhibition. I am flattered to have been invited by Peter to work with him on this project. I am also deeply indebted to the superb staff at the Heritage Center Museum, notably Wendell Zercher, Kim Fortney, and Sandy Lane for their help along the way.

For their enormous assistance, I would like also to express my sincere appreciation to Joel Alderfer of the Mennonite Historians of Eastern Pennsylvania, Cory Amsler of the Bucks County Historical Society/Mercer Museum, Susan Bellingham of Dora Lewis Rare Book Room at the University of Waterloo, Helen Booth of the Jordan Historical Museum of The Twenty, Susan Burke of the Joseph Schneider Haus Museum, Dr. Donald F. Durnbaugh, writers and exhibitors Corinne and Russell Earnest, Dr. Peter C. Erb, Paul and Rita Flack, David and Karen Hampel, Donald and Patricia Herr, Clarke Hess, Joan and Victor Johnson, Moe and Janice Johnson, David Johnston, June Lloyd of The Historical Society of York County, Richard S. and Rosemarie B. Machmer, researcher and author Dennis Moyer, Harriet Robbins, Bruce and Linda Shoemaker, Flora and Byron Spencer, Sam Steiner of Conrad Grebel College, Carolyn Wenger of the Lancaster Mennonite Historical Society, Dr. Gerald Wertkin of the Museum of American Folk Art, David Wheatcroft, historian Dr. Don Yoder, and most notably, Pastors Frederick Weiser and Larry Neff, who have extended kindness and inspiration to me over many years. And at Donning Publishing, I am very appreciative of the work done by senior editor Richard Horwege and as well as Jan Martin and Lori Wiley. Closer to home, I would like to acknowledge the warm support of my family, and the special contribution of Susan Hyde as wife, scholar, and continual inspiration.

In the world of *fraktur* it may be *Gott Sei Ehre* but in the realm of working on this project it is *thank you* to all kindly mortals who have been endlessly generous and helpful.

PREFACE

A DEDICATION TO PASTOR FREDERICK S. WEISER

The course of Pennsylvania German *fraktur* scholarship has been a long one, with many twists and turns since the earliest-known treatment of the subject in 1897. Undoubtedly the roads of investigation and reflection will branch in many directions in the twenty-first century, hopefully without losing sight of that immense plateau of insight provided by one singularly accomplished scholar, Pastor Frederick S. Weiser.

What is particularly impressive about Frederick S. Weiser's contribution is his unique integration of two elements rarely found in historical research encyclopedic comprehensiveness and particular innovativeness. Perhaps this is not a particularly daunting task to anyone who is simultaneously competent as reader, digger, lawyer, cleric, detective, handwriting forensics specialist, paper analyst, translator, theologian, musician, historian, and interpreter.

He has been all of these and more, and especially noteworthy is the ongoing generosity which he has extended to the present writer. I am privileged to be among those to whom he has been a taskmaster, teacher, and friend.

I would like to think that the following pages have benefited not only from the Pastor Weiser's insistence upon exactitude of detail but even more from that sense of balance which he brings to the study of Pennsylvania German material culture, and especially *fraktur*. This balance is to be seen in the amalgamation of seriousness and delight in the world which is the subject of these highly diverse texts. Many are the Lutheran and Reformed *Taufschein* texts which were lost, discarded, or even buried with the dead, obscuring the fact that originally they substantially exceeded the numbers of *Vorschrift* specimens or religious texts which have survived in Mennonite and Schwenkfelder communities. For this reason, we draw attention to the smallness of these latter communities in proportion to the overall Pennsylvania German population, and wish to emphasize the importance of *Taufschein* texts as well as *Vorschrift* texts as cultural and religious expressions.

Echoing Pastor Weiser's exhortations to take note of the balanced perspective emanating from the texts and images of *fraktur*, the observer is invited witness here the portrayals of a world is at once disconcerting and uplifting. We encounter here a world which is, to be certain, a gloomy place of vice and temptation, but also a place of joy, beauty, and meaningfulness. The world which threatens to divert the soul away from its divine goal is also the world which grows green to the glory of God. The heart which must contemplate its timely end is, after all, a noble one, grounded in a divine wellspring of goodness.

For the sheer beauty of his scholarship and the delight of his friendship, I would like to express my most profound indebtedness and appreciation to Pastor Frederick S. Weiser.

Figure 1: Johannes Spangenberg. Presentation inscription for pulpit Bible, circa 1770.
A *fraktur* with a specific religious context is this two-page composition made by Johannes Spangenberg for the pulpit Bible given by the Reverend Michael Schlatter to the Reformed Congregation of Easton, Northampton County. (Courtesy of the First United Church of Christ, Easton, Pennsylvania)

INTRODUCTION

RELIGION, ART, AND PENNSYLVANIA GERMAN FRAKTUR

Pennsylvania German folk art is neither Plato's ideal nor Daguerre's mirror....
—Frederick Weiser, "Fraktur," p. 234

Visual beauty reminds the viewer of his home....
—Margaret Miles, p. 143

How fleeting is human time, how man hurries to eternity.
—Ambrosii Lobwasser, *Vermehrt und Vollständiges Gesang-Buch*,
printed by Christoph Saur at Germantown, Pennsylvania, 1763

Intimations of the divine, which is eternal, and imagery of the world, which is temporal—such are the allusions of texts and visual imagery in the more religious examples of Pennsylvania German *fraktur*. In its aesthetic appeal and artistic beauty, which have long attracted the attention of admirers of our folk art, it may sometimes come as a surprise that the subjects treated in *fraktur* range from practical daily exhortations to darker reflections upon the nature and destiny of the soul. It will be the contention of the present discussion and gathering of *fraktur* specimens that whatever this art has to say about God and humanity, it generally keeps an eye focused upon the somber fact of mortality and the urgency of time in preparing for life in the world to come. Whether these texts and images were reflected upon by their makers and recipients is a matter difficult to determine, given the practicality and labor-oriented life-style of rural Pennsylvania Germans. It is clear that *fraktur* images most certainly did not occupy the central place held by Byzantine icons at home or in places of worship. The opportunities for reverential gaze and reflection were surely uncommon, and the sensibility of German Protestantism was far removed from the incarnational theology and liturgical life of the Catholic world in both its Roman and Byzantine manifestations.

The Pennsylvania German churches and sectarians were certainly not without their own religious focal points of reflection, however. Prominent religious themes were grounded in preaching, poular household devotional books and hymnody, sources which increasingly held much common ground among the various groups with the surge of Pietistic spirituality making its presence felt in the later eighteenth and early nineteenth centuries. Classical distinctions between "Church" and "sectarian" theology were blurred significantly by the wave of subjective religious sentiment which washed back and forth across the fertile valleys of Pennsylvania German culture. While certain Anabaptist subjects such as believer's baptism and pacifist outlook can be detected in some earlier hymns, these and other identifying theological positions evaporated from the hymnody appearing in new songbooks adopted after the turn of the nineteenth century. Indeed, the new collections of hymns in the various religious groups came increasingly to resemble one another, dominated by the inward, cross-confessional religiosity of Pietism. It is perhaps no accident that the theme of death and the popularity of Pietism would attain such prominence in hymnody and *fraktur* texts. Given the Pietistic theme of the personal identity of the believer with the life and death of Jesus, the religious outlook of Pietism offered emotional comfort to the soul on earth, anticipating that day which must come to all while living in hope of reunification with Jesus in the Kingdom of Heaven. The title of this study is taken in the seriousness of its fuller expression: *O Noble Heart Consider Thy End*—an injunction found in both *fraktur* and Pennsylvania needlework continually reminding the maker or recipient or keeper of such texts that nothing on this side of Paradise escapes this dire fact, while at the same time maintaining the ultimacy of hope beyond that inevitability.

Religion and Art: Some Historical Reflections

The implicit connection between religion and art has an early theological articulation in the question posed by John of Damascus, who asked, "Is it not natural to want to express the intangible world in images?" To John's question, with its implied *yes*, we might proceed to the subsequent question of why such artistic expression is "natural," or somehow an intrinsic element of human experience.

For our purposes, we might consider a two-level approach to the religion-art connection. At one level there is the broad question of the relation of artistic expression and religious experience generally; at a second level, we might dare to explore the more particular matter of the religion and art of a specific culture—in this case that of the Pennsylvania Germans—maintaining a cautious awareness of a considerable inner diversity within that loosely defined ethos.

Soli Deo Gloria/Gott Sei Ehre

Occasionally, makers of *fraktur* have inscribed Latin or German terms of spiritual reference. In the vast majority of examples, however, artists provide no such explicit dedications, even when texts are taken from biblical or devotional sources, or when images sometimes appear to have symbolic significance. In still other cases, *fraktur* seems to have little religious association at all, and would seem to more decorative than spiritual. And now and then there is the *fraktur* text which is unabashedly earthy or scandalous in its message.

In the ensuing discussion we shall explore the proposition that *fraktur* as an artistic phenomenon possesses religious significance as an indirect manifestation of spiritual sensibilities rooted in longstanding Christian understandings of mortality and hereafter, sin and redemption, abiding eternal values and practical everyday advice, and reflections upon earthly life as a spiritual journey. In some cases the expression is not always even all that indirect, where texts amount to forthright religious instruction, even serving as a Protestant catechism of sorts.

The Latin *Soli Deo Gloria* and the German *Gott Sei Ehre* are kindred dedications, but are not exact translations. The former bears the tone of exclusivity, the latter leaving open the possibility that those acts which honor God also serve the needs of humanity. Both are included in the title in order to emphasize an ongoing theme in the present discussion, namely that explicitly religious and indirectly spiritual motivations co-exist in the world of *fraktur*. While a comparatively small body of *fraktur* seems to have been consciously consecrated to God within an ecclesiastical context (e.g., the richly illuminated manuscripts produced in the Ephrata Cloisters), a vastly larger range of such artistic expression celebrated the beauty of a world understood as divinely created and ordered.

On Art and Religion: Some General Considerations

A broader consideration of the spiritual motivations of artistic expression invites reflection on the variant meanings of the term *religion* itself. It may be helpful, then, to recognize a double-level understanding in the common use of the words *religion* and *religions*. The first term implies universality, the second, particularity. *Religion* derives meaning from the Latin *religio* or *religare*, connoting simply a sense of bondedness or connectedness. In this sense, to be "religious" is to be bound to another reality, the content of which may be infinitely variable. The emphasis is in this case of a personal kind, defining one's spirituality in terms of a connection of Self to Other, the latter being potentially as diverse as God, YHWH, Brahman, Highest Principle, First Mover, Infinite Knowledge, Ultimate Good, or Absolute Beauty. The awareness of this ontological link to a meaningful greater reality may occur within familiar religious communities, but may be experienced also outside such contexts. Hermann Hesse, in his much read *Siddhartha*, depicted one such spiritual pilgrim when he had his protagonist travel in and out of religious communities and traditional belief systems, only to eventually find his religious link to be with his as yet undefined inner self. And the discovery of that link, that experience of *religio*, was to be perceived in the visible landscape, in the image of his face reflected in the waters of the river by which he sits in a state of apparent resignation. Like the drawn or painted image, the reflection in the water "reminded him of his home." It is this *religio* of the human condition which is at the center of countless stories of discovery and transformation: Moses sees a burning bush, Saul is blinded and thrown from his horse, Muhammed has ecstatic visions in a cave, Buddha "wakes up" beneath the bo tree—and in Pennsylvania, Conrad Beissel is inspired to come to Ephrata. All of these are grounded in the discovery of a profound connectedness to an unexpected reservoir of strength and meaning. In these instances, the religious dimension is defined as a bondedness of subject and object, and may come to expression in endlessly variable contexts, inside or outside familiar contours of religious institution and community.

The second consideration of "religion" is a more concrete kind, defined in terms of faith communities themselves. To be religious in this sense is to be defined by entrance into existing religions, e.g., Judaism, Christianity, Islam, Hinduism, Buddhism, indigenous native religions, or other communities shaped by tradition, faith, and practice. In the stories told by Jewish novelist Chaim Potok characters find themselves continually challenged to find and fulfill their personal aspirations in the intellectual world of arts and sciences, while yet retaining or redefining their Jewish religious identities. It is important in Potok's *The Chosen* for young Danny Saunders to discover that his choice of a worldly career as a psychologist will not ultimately contradict his Jewish religious calling, and indeed, he reflects upon the fact that in a deeper way he will continue even to be defined as a rabbi, albeit in secular guise. In a similarly compelling way, the young boy in Potok's *My Name is Asher Lev*, finds himself initially torn between the choices of artistic and religious calling, only to learn eventually that the two can meaningfully inhabit each other.

This twofold consideration of "religion" brings us back to the task of undertaking a discussion of religious art in general, and of the religious significance of *fraktur* and Pennsylvania German folk art. The narrower context entails a consideration of *fraktur* as "Christian" (or more particularly as "Protestant") or even more denominationally as "Church-type" or "plain community." Finer distinctions as to Lutheran, Reformed, Ephrata, Moravian, Schwenkfelder, Mennonite, or Amish introduce still greater challenges to the advocates of categorizing. Even Linnaeus might well have found himself sorely taxed by this sorting prospect.

Examining the subject, on the other hand, in terms of the broader context, is a prospect already suggested by the inner dynamics of Pennsylvania German religious culture. This dynamic is most dramatically encountered in the tug-of-war between the particularizing tendencies of specific denominational confessions and the broadening tendencies of Pietism (sometimes called "heart religion") a religious movement which subordinated ecclesiastical affiliation to personal conversion and "direct" religious experience through individual devotion to Jesus.

In effect, the twofold consideration of "religion" in the universal juxtaposition of "religion and religions" will be seen to maintain its existence in microcosmic form within Pennsylvania German life, with its unresolved tension between denominational community and personal individuation.

Religion and Art: Universal Considerations

Aristotle himself, never a great lover of art and who in fact banned art from the Republic, seems to have recognized the inseparable human motivation toward artistic expression. That he perceived an intrinsic connection between spiritual and artistic drives is suggested in his observation that "the soul never thinks without an image" (Eck, *Darsan*, p. 20 [the reference is to Rudolf Arnheim who is in fact quoting Aristotle]). Was Aristotle unusually insightful of the interesting fact that art does indeed flourish even in those religious traditions which discourage religious artistic expression? Jewish historian Cecil Roth has produced a beautiful volume of Jewish art even though prefaced by a disclaimer that Judaism has historically discouraged the rendering of religious images. In an Islamic context, Baktiar and Ardalan have produced *The Sense of Unity: The Sufi Tradition in Persian Architecture*, a study of the geometric and abstract artistic means by which Muslim artists have used art in the service of divine praise, even though Islamic tradition has eschewed religious art. Some accounts of Mennonite and Amish culture in North America have characterized these traditions as anti-iconic, in keeping with the tenets of a "plain people" at the same time that there is an abundant library of books, exhibitions, and catalogues of Mennonite and Amish decorative arts (notable examples are at the Heritage Center of Lancaster, and also at the Joseph Schneider Haus Museum in Kitchener, Ontario). In numerous traditions, proscriptions against religious artistic expression have not succeeded in preventing the emergence of a religious art, but perhaps have served only to occasion the transmutation of art into symbolic, geometric, or other indirect modes of expression. In Judaism, the picture of the God in heaven was at early date replaced by the hand from the sky; in Islam, the idea of the active Allah is denied pictorial representation but nonetheless is hinted in the endlessly moving arabesque; in many traditions, the picture of God creating the world gives way to the stylized depiction of the created world of birds, flowers, and trees.

The universal inclination toward artistic expressiveness, and especially toward religious-artistic expressiveness, may indeed have its roots in the aforesaid notion of *religio* as bondedness, since "bondedness" implies a separation between one's present existence and one's potential place. The tension is expressed in countless cultures as the experience of loneliness, a separation from one's place of origin, or, alternatively from one's place of destiny. In her study of religion and visual art, *Image as Insight: Visual Understanding in Western Christianity and Secular Culture*, Margaret Miles cites the Platonic way of putting the situation, that "visual beauty reminds the viewer of his home" (p. 143). To the degree that human consciousness entertains questions about origins and destinations, it might reasonably be argued that artistic expression is no less sensitive to this underlying experience of separation and potential connectedness. Similarly, it might be argued that the artistic process itself—the application of color and texture, the construction of pattern, design, and form—are means by which chaos is transformed or tamed, and order is wrought from disorder. Formlessness becomes world. When those incurable decorators of the domestic habitat whom we call yard artists create arrangements of wood, plastic, plaster, and cement on their lawns, could not the instinct for order be as paramount as the easily attributed motives of attention-seeking or mischievous humor? Is it much of a logical step to attribute similar instinctive forces in the symmetries of *fraktur* and related folk art? Historian of religion Frederick Streng (no relative of *fraktur* artist Christian Strenge) has written that "art is the incarnation of a meaning-producing human being" (*Understanding Religious Man*, p. 84). He argues that artistic activity is religiously significant because it amounts to the "structuring" of the world in comprehensible patterns. Such "structuring," of course, has its primordial counterpart in the creation myths of many world religions. Mircea Eliade, longtime scholar of ancient cultures and their importance for modern-day patterns of living, defines in *The Myth of Eternal Return* any repeated acts as "rituals," further arguing that "every ritual has a divine model, an archetype" (p. 21). For him, repetition is a way of living in an atemporal present (p. 86). That the principle of repetition and of patterning is grounded in an archetypal source seems more easily supportable than the many attempts to link concrete symbols to a Ur-source, as attempted by writers such as John Joseph Stoudt. His analysis of Pennsylvania German folk art is interesting to the degree that he calls attention to the matter of form and design, but this promising attempt to develop a universal, cross-cultural analysis of artistic motivation is all too quickly subordinated to his greater emphasis upon symbols and divine prototypes. Although he offers an initial caution about prejudging the motivations of Pennsylvania artists and scriveners, he inevitably ascribes a metaphysical consciousness with little evidence offered to demonstrate such overt intentionality. It is no wonder, then, that scholars such as Pastor Frederick S. Weiser, who as a committed pastor and hence no stranger to theological reflection upon the tangible world, finds it necessary to advocate discretion in such enterprises. About symbolism in *fraktur*, he cautions, "looking too deeply for meaning in a *fraktur* pomegranate is as fruitful as analyzing why owls and turtles have center stage on your cocktail napkins and guest towels" (*Fraktur*, p. 7).

Bearing in mind such well-placed cautions, in what sense can we then examine Pennsylvania German folk art and *fraktur* as forms of religious expression? If we find it prudent to abstain from the attribution of explicit religious motivation to the scriveners who drew birds and hearts and tulips on paper, is there still reasonable room for consideration of a religious dimension of an indirect kind?

As a starting point, it would be helpful to make a distinction which Stoudt does not—namely, an acknowledgment that despite the visual similarity of *fraktur* to other manifestations of Pennsylvania German folk expression, it needs to examined *sui generis*. Stoudt's broad analysis of "Pennsylvania German folk art" makes no distinction between the art of *fraktur* from the arts of ceramics, textiles, ironwork, or furniture painting. The presence of a visual image on an earthenware pot or a wooden panel on a chest or as the terminus of a hinge or meat fork does not necessarily function in the same way as a corresponding image in *fraktur*. Indeed, texts on slipware and elsewhere are sometimes earthy enough that they may be best left untranslated for English readers, who might be startled at their earthy content. While the making of *fraktur* is also frequently a domestic art form like the former, in many instances it inhabits a fundamentally different context, produced in the setting of the parochial school or the church or faith community. Furthermore, *fraktur* differs from these other forms of Pennsylvania German folk art in the intrinsic connection which it has long possessed with religious texts. While specific one-to-one correlations of texts and images are admittedly infrequent (see Weiser and Hollyday), there is nevertheless a shared "ethos" of text and image which imbues *fraktur* with religious significance, albeit latent and inferred rather than actualized and articulated. For the maker of *fraktur* texts and images, as well as for children who see texts and are given presentation *frakturs* in school, or for parents requesting *fraktur* birth-and-baptismal certificates, or family members reminded of daily spiritual considerations by house blessings seen in the home, *fraktur* could well serve the simple needs of decoration while at the same time "reminding the viewer of his home."

Religious Folk Art in a North American Context

North American soil was fertile ground for the transplanting of established European religions or the incubation of new religions. The imagery of a New England, New Spain, or New France was an alluring one for those thousands of immigrants arriving in North American shores in the sixteenth and seventeenth centuries and afterwards. Many were the German-speaking Protestants who entered Pennsylvania through Germantown after 1683 and others who settled further north in the Lunenburg area of Nova Scotia after 1750.

While the focus of the present discussion is upon the specific phenomenon of *fraktur* as a form of folk art expression among the Pennsylvania Germans, it seems worthy of brief consideration to acknowledge the greater context of religious folk art in North America, especially as it had reached its flowering in the eighteenth and nineteenth centuries.

The body of religious folk art was to take on several diverse cultural cloaks during this time frame, represented principally in the four transplanted traditions of the Spanish, French, English, and German cultures growing up in what have become the national contexts of Mexico, Canada, and the United States. In each of these regions folk art flourished in ways that reflect the distinctiveness of religious life and practice, ranging from the highly church-focused religious communities of Roman Catholic French and Spanish America to the more diffused Protestant ethos of English and German regions of settlement.

Parallels: Religious Folk Art in French, Spanish, and English North America

Religious Folk Art: French North America

In French North America, the beginnings of an indigenous arts tradition can probably be dated from the seventeenth century, when Bishop Laval established an arts-and-crafts school at Saint-Joachim, about thirty miles south of Montreal. Its teachers and journeymen practitioners produced work in continuity with the high-art traditions of the French homeland, providing furnishings, sculpture, and paintings for the new churches of the colonists along the St. Lawrence River. The early works, one step removed from the sophistication of European workshops, provided a material focal point for lesser-trained craftsmen and inspired amateurs who carved or painted religious subjects for home use. In the nineteenth century (and continuing into the twentieth), in part due to expansion and new construction, and in part to the impact of waves of religious piety felt throughout French Catholicism in North America, there was a great flowering of religious folk art throughout that region of Lower Canada eventually to be known as the province of Quebec.

Folk art in French North America possessed several distinguishing features. It was largely a Roman Catholic art, with emphasis on strongly sacramental themes, notably the centrality of the Eucharist, emphasizing its motifs of bread and wine, paten and chalice, host and monstrance. The image of the Crucifixion was equally important, and held an intrinsic association with the Eucharist and Liturgy of the Mass, by which it was continually remembered and celebrated. The Crucifixion appears in countless small crosses made for the walls and bedside tables of homes, and, on a larger scale, as roadside Crucifixes serving as places of devotion throughout the countryside.

French Canadian religious folk art tended to be strongly pictorial in character, whether in plastic (sculptural) or two-dimensional form (paintings and drawings). Among the earliest surviving examples of French folk art in North America are *ex-votos*, or paint-

Figure 2: John Adam Eyer. Text for Jacob Meyer, 1780 (26 cm. x 21 cm., 10.75" x 8.25"). Occasionally *fraktur* artists made use of familiar Latin texts. This elaborate reward of merit for Jacob Meyer, "first foresinger" in the Perkasie School at Hilltown in Bucks County, bears the praise *Soli Deo Gloria*. Such stock phrases may have been taken more seriously by schoolmasters than recipients, but they do suggest something of the religious dimension of teaching in the denominational schools of the time. (Courtesy of the Jordan Historical Museum of the Twenty)

ings of thanksgiving, notable manifestations of which are dated from as early as 1697 to around 1760. Such paintings were typically executed by their makers as an act of gratitude for a petition granted. Well-known Quebec examples depict miraculous interventions bringing about recovery from illness or rescue from a shipwreck or fire or other calamity. There are no known sculptural *ex-votos* in the French tradition in America, but more than a dozen painted forms are known.

Another highly popular subject in French Canada was the Holy Family, with many sculptures and painted images of Mary, Joseph, and the Christ Child. Folk artists also carved small statues of a small number of saints and angels, largely inspired by wood and (later) plaster figures in the side altars of parish churches. In this regard, it would probably be fair to say that the context for French folk art in North America was largely ecclesiastical, particularly in consideration of the extent to which folk artists drew their inspiration largely from the altar crosses, sculptures, and paintings seen in village churches. Their works took the forms of paintings, sculptures, and tableaux, reflecting both the learned theology of official Church and the grass-roots outlook and practice of popular piety.

Religious Folk Art: Spanish North America

Like life further to the north in eastern Canada, the transplanted Catholic Church set the tone of artistic expression in Mexico and those regions eventually to come into the framework of California and the American Southwest. The establishment of the Church in Mexico predates even that of French Canada, while great blossoming of religious folk art seems to have reached its zenith in the nineteenth and early twentieth centuries.

The conquest of Mexico in the early 1500s was marked by a vigorous program of conversion and building of churches. The spread of the Catholic faith was undertaken primarily by orders—the Dominicans, Franciscans, Jesuits, and others.

The folk art of New Spain, like that of New France, was strongly Roman Catholic in content, with ecclesiastical art and sculpture providing a wealth of imagery for self-taught artists. While Spanish folk art concentrated upon Eucharistic images, in similar fashion to that of French Canada, there was a profound difference of atmosphere. The lighter themes of salvation and thanksgiving in the sacrament of the Eucharist were for the most part overshadowed in Mexico and (later) the American Southwest by the darker intonations of sin and repentance central to the sacrament of Penance. Reflecting a medieval preoccupation (which lasted longer in Spain than in other parts of Europe) with the imitation of Jesus' human suffering as the sinner's means of attaining remission of the punishment of sin, Mexican popular religion was permeated through and through with images of the broken and wounded body of Jesus. Sculptures of the bleeding Jesus, or even skeleton figures, were paraded in religious processions during Holy Week, and these images appeared widely in the work of amateur woodcarvers and painters.

The range of subjects treated by Mexican and Hispanic-American painters was much more diverse than in Canada, with depictions of the life and miracles or several dozens of saints, in addition to pictures of the Holy Family and well-known biblical scenes. Votive art was perhaps even more popular in New Spain than in New France, and took for the form of sculpture as well as painted image. The painted *ex-voto* continued to be popular in Mexico and parts of the American Southwest into the twentieth century, more than two centuries after it had disappeared as an art form in French Canada.

Figure 3. Abraham Schultz. Bookplate, 1786 (15.6 cm. x 9.6 cm., 6" x 3.75").
Attributed to Schwenkfelder catechetical instructor Abraham Schultz (1747–1822), this bookplate was made for the catechism of Andreas Schultz in Upper Hanover Township, Montgomery County. The text concludes with the Latin praise, *Gloria in excelsis Deo.*
(Courtesy of the Schwenkfelder Library and Heritage Center)

Religious Folk Art: English North America, New England, and the Atlantic Seaboard

Because the earliest period of English settlement in America was defined largely by the predominance of Puritans in the Massachusetts colony, there is a common tendency to suggest that artistic expression was not a part of this austere cultural tradition. This rumor is quickly put to rest, of course, upon even a casual examination of the material culture of seventeenth and eighteenth century America, where one comes immediately upon the existence of indigenous furniture (carved and painted), textile arts, and decorated tombstones. While many writers (Increase Mather in his biography of Richard Mather; Perry Miller in *The Puritans*; Charles Bergengren's "'Finished to the Utmost Nicety': Plain Portraits in America, 1760–1860," in Vlach and Bronner's *Folk Art and Art Worlds*) have made mention of the Puritan emphasis upon "plain style," it would be erroneous to take plain style to mean no style. Simplicity of style can in itself constitute an aesthetic, in this case an aesthetic in keeping with the religious principle of subordinating material priorities to spiritual ones.

That there is a measurable correlation between religion and folk art expression in New England is suggested by James Deetz in his important study of carved tombstones, *In Small Things Forgotten*. Deetz argues that tombstone decoration in Massachusetts underwent stylistic changes, in step with religious changes in the colony. From a first stage of Puritan orthodoxy in which decoration emphasized the theme of death through the motif of winged skulls carved on burial stones, there emerged a softening of Puritan doctrine and practice, accompanied by a transformation of the skulls to winged cherubs. By mid-century, not only Puritanism in particular but religion in general was marginalized by the secularizing tendencies of the time, reflected in new neoclassical styles and the prevalence of willows and urns in tombstone decoration.

The centrality of Christian theology was perpetuated in schools, where engraved images in primers frequently served as a basis for drawings and paintings of religious subjects done by self-taught artists on the Atlantic seaboard. Such images were found in the margins of hand-lettered birth and family records, in folded-paper "puzzles" based upon the story of the Fall of Adam and its consequences, or in compositions serving as pictures in their own right. An especially prominent setting for religious content in New England decorative arts was the embroidered sampler, done at home and taught in schools for girls. Samplers had the potential of speaking to both the epigraphic and visual aesthetic, since many combined verses with images, frequently exhorting the viewer to reflection upon the higher realities.

In other religious groups within the Anglo-American culture, folk art expression was sometimes the work of an individual or small group of artist-visionaries, but nevertheless could be said to reflect wider religious impulses in the community at large. Such is the case with regard to the "spirit drawings" done by a small number of individuals in the Hancock Shaker Community in western New York State and elsewhere. The visionary aspect of many of these drawings has led some writers to describe them as depictions of the wonders of Heaven, as in *Visions of the Heavenly Sphere: A Study in Shaker Religious Art* by Edward and Faith Andrews. While the number of artists who produced these remarkable drawings is very small, the inspiration from the surrounding Shaker culture is evident, particularly with respect to the promotion of ecstatic visions through ritual dance and meetings of the community. Here a "plain culture" promotes an external appearance of austere style while at the same time permitting ritual observance and practice which in effect become a catalyst for visual artistic expression.

In another setting, Quaker artist Edward Hicks (1780–1849) painted many versions of *The Peaceable Kingdom*, adapted from an engraving, itself an image of a painting by Richard Westall. Hicks added another borrowed detail—this time from Benjamin West—the scene of William Penn making payment and pledging a treaty of peace with Indians in return for lands acquired for newly arriving European settlers. While Shaker theology advised simplicity and plainness in all aspects of life, its emphasis upon brotherhood and peaceful means was the religious content which Penn was to set forth in visual terms over a period of nearly thirty years. It would not be an undue exaggeration perhaps to suggest that Hicks painted on canvas what Quakers felt in their hearts.

"Plain" cultures are like teakettles, in that while all is seemingly smooth on the surface, there do have to be openings somewhere to release that which is stirring below. Like rising steam, the urge to beautify one's surroundings invariably finds its way to the surface where it bursts forward into plain view.

In those areas of British settlement, overwhelmingly Protestant in religious character, there is little in the way of an official religious art. Unlike the carvers and painters of New France and New Spain, those in New England rarely found occasion to produce work for the church or for sacramental or devotional practice transferred from church to home. Religious sentiments had to find more indirect means of expression, through textile arts, tombstone carving, and occasional graphic representations in keeping with the texts and music and other observances of the religious communities in which such artists lived. The visual arts of Anglo-American culture were not particularly ecclesiastical in function or appearance, but were no less religiously significant as expressions of belief and value within a diversified Protestant ethos.

Religious Folk Art Among the Pennsylvania Germans

The early German settlements of Pennsylvania comprised what was essentially a Protestant culture, with a sprinkling of Catholic and Jewish groups within the larger population. This German Protestant culture bespeaks of remarkable internal diversity, ranging from the more stalwart doctrinal, ecclesiastical, and sacramental orthodoxy of Lutheran and Reformed Churches on the one hand to the various Anabaptist groups of Mennonites, Amish, and others with their emphasis on "believer's baptism" and upon pacifist principles. The Schwenkfelders shared much of the outlook of Mennonites. Moravians saw themselves as a spiritual community which might harmonize the various Pennsylvania religious groups, and the Ephrata Cloisters retained its distinctive identity as the only early American Protestant cloistered community. The distinguishing marks of the various denominations were not always as sharply defined, especially in the fact of the more universalizing religious phenomena of mysticism and pietism, the latter whose sentiments find expression in the hymnody and *fraktur* texts of every group.

With regard to Pennsylvania German *fraktur*, Don Yoder has described it at one level as "a religious art," and then, at a second, "as a Protestant art." For Yoder the Protestant character of Pennsylvania German folk is that it is "Word-centered," reflecting a Protestant emphasis upon the text, the sermon, and music as acoustic rather than visual means of expression.

In notable contrast to the relative scarcity of painted and drawn religious imagery in English-speaking areas of Protestant North America, the arts of the Pennsylvania Germans manifest themselves in a visual display which is ubiquitous among the various denominations and subcultures within this Germanic Protestant culture. The earliest forms of *fraktur* from illuminated texts produced within the Ephrata Cloisters to baptismal certificates and *Vorschrift* texts tend to appear in conjunction with the printed word, even when there is no apparent direct linkage between image and text. Stand-alone drawn images, emerging perhaps in earliest form as presentation gifts from teachers to pupils, become increasingly common by mid-nineteenth century and in the closing decades of hand-drawn *fraktur* production. Even here, images are frequently derived from printed certificates in which printed texts of birth and baptism had been prominent.

The explosion of artistic expression in the form of *fraktur* gives Pennsylvania German folk art a readily observable distinct quality which stands it in marked contrast to the visual arts of New England and English-speaking areas of the Mid-Atlantic region. The recurring motifs used by *fraktur* artists have their in-house parallels to other decorative traditions brought from the Swiss-German background, including painted furniture, embroidered textiles, decorated ceramics, and carved tombstones. The specific practice of *fraktur* can be seen to have earlier European origins, particularly in schools where teachers made *Vorschriften* and in religious contexts where sponsors hand-lettered texts were presented along with gifts to children on the occasion of church baptisms.

The matter of defining the religious dimension of Pennsylvania German *fraktur* is an arena in which many voices have been heard and will no doubt continue to do so. While significant differences are much in evidence, it is significant that within the considerable range of perspectives there is to be found in virtually every contribution to the discussion an acknowledgement of a spiritual dimension in the imagery and frequently in the process itself. Not everyone shares Joseph Stoudt's inclination to amalgamate religion and psychoanalysis, as in his claim that the decorative motifs and geometric designs in *fraktur* are rooted in universal unconscious archetypes. Many writers do give credit to Stoudt, however, for his emphasis upon the importance of observing connections between visual imagery and the rich literary background of scriptural and devotional texts read or in various ways known in Pennsylvania German households and schools. Cautioning against giving too much weight to writing, reading, or hearing of the printed word, Pastor Fred Weiser warns that these "highly religious texts cannot be taken at face value as if every Dutchmen spent his life on his knees" (Weiser, "Fraktur," p. 234). Christa Pieske suggests that printed texts were indeed important in daily life, particularly with regard to printed broadsides with pictures (*bilderbogen*), whose function was "to communicate religious ideas, to teach by means of moral or ethical maxims" (Pieske, "The European Origins . . . ," p. 7). In the same sentence Pieske indicates that these broadsides served also an "entertainment" function. It would seem that moral seriousness and sunnier enjoyments need not be separated from one another.

Pennsylvania German culture was by no means a homogeneous phenomenon, not even when that surging wave of religious sentiment described loosely as Pietism threatened to undercut denominational and theological distinctions. *Fraktur* expression seems to have been a form of visual expression which flourished in every corner of southeastern Pennsylvania, reflecting what Don Yoder terms "different centers of gravity." Pennsylvania *fraktur* in its earliest incarnation was produced in the cloisters of Ephrata in a manner almost reminiscent of the medieval scriptorium. In Lutheran and Reformed communities it was to be seen in countless variations of *Taufschein* recording church baptisms, while in Mennonite schools it assumed the format of the *Vorschrift* with its religious text and "practical" elements of numerals and alphabets. Weiser indicates that the time was not long before the religious significance of baptismal witnessing was lost and the *Taufschein* came eventually to amount more to a record of birth than testimony of baptism. Still, it continued for many decades to retain its highly formalized texts attesting to the role of the faith community in the journey of the soul from the darkness of infancy to the light of salvation. For Robert Mickey, the widespread popularity of these various forms indicates both the diversity of religious outlook (e.g., the variety of maxims extolled in *Vorschriften*) and the uniformity of ecclesiastical precepts (e.g., the formality of *Taufschein*) (Mickey, p. 16). Dennis Moyer's reflection upon the significance of this mode of Pennsylvania German expression is quite explicitly theistic in its emphasis: "Fraktur is an art that grew from a love of God and respect for God's Word" (Moyer, p. 2). Seemingly we have come to the opposite end of the spectrum when we consider the more earthly assessment by Frederick Weiser, when he suggests that the folk decoration on *fraktur* texts "reveals sheer delight with the world and its things, both natural and man-made" (Weiser, "Fraktur," p. 234). Elsewhere, Pastor Weiser has faintly acknowledged some legitimacy to the search for transcendental references in folk, allowing that "perhaps in a general way the combination of flowing design and bright colors is a depiction of heaven's glories," but he then immediately warns against the dangers of "looking too deeply . . ." (Weiser, *Fraktur*, p. 7).

One might be inclined to follow this argument to its end and then perhaps even beyond, to consider the possibility that in the religious outlook of many of the Pennsylvania German communities the world was in fact a decidedly improper place to search for religious meaning.

To be certain, there is much in hymnody and literature in the various Pennsylvania German communities to issue a danger signal, namely that the world in its allurements must never be permitted to distract the believer from the true prize of the Kingdom of God. At worst, the presence of *Ecclesiastes* and its warning that indulgence in the pleasures of the world may constitute the ultimate hybris ("vanity of vanities") can sometimes be found even in *fraktur* texts themselves. At other times, the world is an ephemeral place, or a vale of tears from which the spiritual pilgrim longs for release through death, a theme found frequently in the texts of the *Notenbüchlein* made by John Adam Eyer and other teachers in various schools at the end of the eighteenth and beginning of the nineteenth centuries. To be sure, the visible world is an ambiguous place for the seeker of that infinite place beyond material appearances.

Nonetheless, there is another side to all of this. The world of natural and even humanly constructed beauty is never pronounced evil, a judgment that would hardly be consistent with the biblical account of creation and the making of a "world and its things" deemed to be good. Perhaps the "sheer delight with the world and its things" to which Pastor Weiser makes reference is not an exclusive domain, segregated somehow from the world divinely created and hence a manifestation of divine providence, no less than humanity which, even in its fallen form, remains *imago dei*, the world and its things retain vestiges of that divine world to which they refer, however obliquely. This "sheer delight" in the world does not, by any stretch of the imagination, require forgetfulness of its spiritual ground. The insight is expressed most capably in the text of an 1817 *fraktur* by Andreas Kolb found in Weiser and Heaney's *The Pennsylvania German Fraktur of the Free Library of Philadelphia*, fig. 234:

How many pretty little flowers
one sees at springtime. . . .

Everything grows green
to the honour of God

Figure 4: Photograph. Ephrata Cloister.
Photograph of the meeting-house (*Saal*), one of the surviving buildings from the Ephrata Cloister which flourished from 1735 to 1800, and later through its colony cloister at Snow Hill, Pennsylvania. The first systematic production of *fraktur* in America took place in the scriptorium of the Ephrata Cloister. A principal incentive was the determination to provide illuminated pages and margins for the various collections of hymns gathered, composed, and printed under the leadership of Conrad Beissel. In short time, the Ephrata printing press was in demand by various groups for the printing of their devotional texts and hymnals, and by the 1780s was engaged in the printing of *Taufschein* forms used for the recording of births and baptisms in Lutheran and Reformed communities. (Michael Bird Photo)

CHAPTER I

CONTEXTS: TAUFSCHEIN, VORSCHRIFT, AND OTHER TEXTS

In speaking of religious contexts for *fraktur*, it is necessary by way of a brief prolegomenon to acknowledge that not all *fraktur* was made in institutional contexts. Such is the case with regard to modest drawings made at home, or for family or friends. Domestic and personal, rather than institutional contexts would be evident in the work of later artists such as Barbara Ebersol (1846–1922) in Pennsylvania or Anna Weber (1814–1888) in Ontario, who produced many bookplates and pictures for family, relatives, and friends. Similar contexts may have occasioned also the earlier work of artists such as David Herr (active 1820s) in Lancaster County. In such examples, there is little textual or contextual corroboration to suggest more overtly religious motivations. Our attention is drawn, however, to a different category of work which can be associated with institutional and religious settings. In these contexts, the content of the works produced can be said to express—even proclaim—the spiritual or moral axioms of the contexts engendering the *fraktur* specimens in question.

The two most prominent *fraktur* forms defined by institutional contexts are the *Taufschein* and the *Vorschrift*. The former is a text which records—perhaps even "witnesses"—the sacramental event of entry into the Christian community, while the latter is also a text, expressing a scriptural, devotional, or moral axiom in the traditional format of the motto. The *Taufschein* is essentially documentary while the *Vorschrift* is didactic. The *Taufschein* had its home in the "Church" community of rural Pennsylvania (e.g., Lutheran and Reformed), while the *Vorschrift* flourished in the "plain" community, primarily Mennonite and Schwenkfelder. In its Lutheran or Reformed contexts, the *Taufschein* served the young child, the *Vorschrift* was made for the young pupil (eight to twelve years old). The *Taufschein* functioned within the Church, where it was associated with the act of baptism, whereas the *Vorschrift* functioned within the school, where it was connected with the process of religious and moral education.

The text of the *Taufschein* is religious, attesting to the Church's instrumental role in admitting the infant into the community of salvation. Even the naming of the child is the function of the Church, the name being "given" by the pastor in the act of baptizing the child. Typically, the text of the *Taufschein* is conventionalized and ritualized, its contents comprising the following: name of child, place and date of birth, date of baptism, names of parents, names of witnesses, name of presiding clergy, place of baptism and/or name of church, doctrinal affirmation of significance of baptism as entry in the Christian faith and as the door of salvation. Decorative motifs are enormously varied, and may have occasional connection to the content of the text, although specific correlations are comparatively rare.

Figure 5: Anonymous. Illumination ("Resurrection Diptych") for Johann Conrad Beissel, *Paradisisches Wunder Spiel*, circa 1754.
Numerous illuminations accompany texts on pages of the *Wunder Spiel*, a collection of hymns for the early cloister at Ephrata. The Resurrection is an important theme in the religious outlook of Ephrata texts and music, especially as they reflect the theology of Jacob Boehme as interpreted by Conrad Beissel. Boehme linked Resurrection and Last Judgment, a time at which the human soul would be united with Jesus (the New Adam) in the "Marriage of the Lamb." The object of spiritual life was diligent preparation for this union of the earthly bride with the mystical bridegroom. (Courtesy of the Winterthur Library: Joseph Downs Collection of Manuscripts and Printed Ephemera, No. 65X560)

Figure 6: Anonymous. Illuminated page from *Turteltaube*, 1746 (22.3 cm. x 17 cm., 9" x 6.875").
The mystical imagery of the soul as a lonely turtledove, seeking reunion with Jesus as mystical bridegroom, has its very early expression at Ephrata. In 1746 the community brought forth from its press "The Bitter-Sweet, or Song of the Lonely Turtle-Dove, the Christian Church here on Earth. . . ." (Courtesy of the Rare Book Department, Free Library of Philadelphia, No. FLP 1148)

The *Vorschrift*, also a religious text, has a much different purpose from that of the *Taufschein*. It is generally the work of the teacher, some of whom were capable scriveners, and seems to have been presented to pupils by teachers. It has often been said that the *Vorscrhift* was a penmanship model made by the teacher and copied by pupils. While this may sometimes have been the case, actual verifiable reports of this use are not widely known. Signed examples and others attributable on circumstantial grounds make clear that teachers were of diverse or unknown denominational backgrounds, providing instruction for primarily Mennonite pupils. It would appear that the religious content of the *Vorschrift* may have been chosen with some thought given to the religious community, but this should not be overstated, given the wide circulation of texts across denominational lines, especially those expressing Pietistic themes.

The composition of the *Vorschrift* is relatively constant, even when examples are studied over the approximately fifty-year period in which the form flourished. The typical *Vorschrift* is comprised of a religious text, more often than not taken from Scripture, followed by a "practical" section with letters of the alphabet and numbers, usually one to twenty. In many instances the texts amount essentially to moral maxims, extolling virtues and guidelines for the proper life of faith. Characteristic of such reminders are axioms such as "Fear of the Lord is the beginning of wisdom" or "Before the time of Judgment examine yourself" or "Diligence in youth is preparation for joy in eternity."

At least one *Vorschrift* has been cited as having a "Church" (Lutheran or Reformed) context, since its text is the Apostles' Creed (Weiser, *The Gift is Small*, p. 23). It is also possible, however, that the schoolmaster/*fraktur* artist who produced this "Creedal" *Vorschrift* may have drawn as easily from "plain" as "Church" sources, since the Apostles' Creed does also appear in several hymnals, including the Mennonite *Liedersammlung*, the *Ausbund*, and the *Unpartheyische Gesangbuch*.

The Vorschrift in the School

It was in the setting of the parochial school that the *Vorschrift* could be said to have been born, raised, and died. It served well the German-language instruction of the eighteenth and early nineteenth-century rural school, and its usefulness eventually disappeared with the introduction of English-language instruction after the mid-1830s.

It has been observed that "the parochial school was the bosom of the phenomenon of Fraktur" (Weiser, "Fraktur," p. 231). The nurturing metaphor is an apt one, of course, pointing to the role of the school in providing for its pupils the essence of Pennsylvania German Protestant education, e.g., knowledge in reading, arithmetic, handwriting and calligraphy, and, of course, religious and moral instruction. Many are the examples of *Vorschriften* which, though written by teachers of several religious backgrounds, were made in the context of Mennonite schools.

It was not only Mennonite pupils who were recipients of *Vorschriften*, however. In a parallel context, the *Vorschrift* appears to have been a fact of life in Schwenkfelder schools in Montgomery County, many of these located in close proximity to Mennonite schools in the same region. Similarities of design in some instances suggest that some Schwenkfelder practitioners were aware of examples made for Mennonite pupils. In his study of *fraktur* in the Schwenkfelder library, Dennis K. Moyer says of Schwenkfelder artist Abraham Heebner (1760–1838) that "he clearly studied under Huppert Cassel" who was probably a Mennonite practitioner (Moyer, p. 68). He also suggests that Susanna Heebner (1750–1818) used floral design motifs derived from Mennonite artist Andreas Kolb (1749–1811) with whom she may have been classmate in the Mennonite parochial school at Skippack prior to the establishment of a Schwenkfelder school at nearby Towamencin (Moyer, p. 75).

While mention has been made of the use of the *Vorschrift* in schools in Mennonite, Reformed, and Lutheran communities, it is interesting to see how the form was utilized and perhaps modified in the schools of another group, namely the Schwenkfelders in Montgomery County. There it seems to have been less popular than a slightly variant form—that is, a religious text without alphabet or numbers. Unlike the *Vorschrift* which sometimes stopped in mid-sentence, the religious text was carefully planned to include the entire citation. Did the *Vorschrift* appear on the scene first, to be followed later by the religious text (rendered more theological by the deletion of the "applied" section), or did the religious text come first, followed by the *Vorschrift* (made more "practical" by the addition of alphabetical and numerical learning tools)? In either sequence, it would seem that the school was an important setting for the inculcation of religious truths, which in these contexts appear to be less doctrinal than ethical. Indeed, to describe the bottom rows of a *Vorschrift* as "practical" may be somewhat remiss, and indeed, doing so may obscure the fact that the choice of scriptural and other texts has a practical aim as well, since many of these texts allude not so much to what one should believe as to what one should do.

The Taufschein: "Church" and "Community" Contexts

Many are the historians who have called attention to the varied makeup of Pennsylvania's diverse religious groups. Within the German-speaking settlements of rural Pennsylvania, a two-fold distinction between "Church" groups and "plain people" has been delineated by scholars as diverse as F. Ernest Stoeffler, Donald Yoder, and Frederick Weiser (cf. discussions in various sections of Stoeffler's *Continental Pietism*; Yoder's *Picture-Bible*; and Weiser's *Fraktur*).

In the German-speaking regions of Pennsylvania, comprised almost entirely of Protestant groups, the church-type would be embodied in institutional form by the Lutheran and German Reformed Churches. The importance of the church to the life and destiny of the individual is here manifested in the sacramental role of the churches and the emphasis consequently placed upon baptism as entry to salvation. Baptism of the individual by the church is regarded as of such saving importance that the sacrament is administered as shortly as possible after birth. To delay baptism would be to place in jeopardy the eternal life of the newborn child. Furthermore, it is baptism which confers upon the recipient its own religious identity, symbolized in the custom of the child receiving its name by the officiating clergy.

The "plain-community type" in Pennsylvania embraces many groups, among them Mennonites, Amish, Brethren, Schwenkfelders, and others. In areas of the western United States and Canada, a different Anabaptist group, the Hutterian Brethren, described themselves with the word *Bruderhof*. These faith communities are notable, at least in theory, for a decentralization of episcopal authority, simplicity of worship, and greater emphasis upon the individual and direct reading of scripture. With regard to baptism, emphasis is shifted from the role of the ecclesiastical institution in administering function to the role of the individual in the decision-making and acceptance of the sacrament. The popular term *believer's baptism* is sometimes used in this case to designate the idea that the baptism is freely entered into by the young adult having reached the "age of reason." The candidate comes forward with an already established identity, retaining the name given by parents at birth.

Differences in baptismal doctrine and practice have important implications for *fraktur* practice in Pennsylvania. The vast majority of *fraktur* birth-and-baptismal certificates were made in Lutheran and Reformed communities, where infant baptism was the norm. Because these documents recorded both birth and baptism, the occasionally close chronological proximity of these two events meant that a scrivener could produce a "full" document at one go. This was particularly true for printed versions, whose formulaic text was prepared in advance, leaving only the task of in-filling the particulars of names and dates. Even artists who lettered and drew their own documents could do the text in advance, then fill in details on the occasion of the child's baptism.

Figure 7: Johannes Bard. Drawing, circa 1820. Architectural subjects sometimes drew the attention of *fraktur* artists. Frederick Weiser has suggested the strong possibility that the structure in this work by Johannes Bard (1797–1861) may be Holy Cross Church in Union Township, Adams County, the place of worship attended by the artist in his youth. (Michael Bird Photo)

It is interesting to observe a phenomenon in which such documents were sometimes made for "plain-type" groups which did not practice infant baptism. In some cases, the logical expectation is that *fraktur* scriveners would produce a "birth-only" document. To be certain, examples of this alternative format are to be found, as in the birth records attributed to Eli Haverstick and Samuel Bentz (figs. 20 and 21), both in the Heritage Center Museum of Lancaster collection. The reality, however, is that the preferred solution was to simply use the church-type *Taufschein* form, leaving blank the space set aside for baptism. Because the interval between birth and baptism among Mennonites and other "believer's baptism" groups often exceeded ten years, it is not surprising that many of the forms used for these groups were never "completed." Examples of these forms are to be seen in hand-drawn birth-and-baptismal forms by Joseph Lochbaum and Christian L. Hoover (figs. 17 and 18).

The existence of "birth-only" records may indicate either of two developments with regard to the religious significance of *fraktur* production. On the one hand, there is a sense in which the activity continues to have theological importance as it reflects a distinction between church-type and plain-community-type views of baptism. On the other hand, as Frederick S. Weiser has pointed out, the "birth-only" certificate may well be the harbinger of cultural things to come, with declining emphasis upon theological witness to baptism and a shift toward the more neutral matter of recordkeeping of births and deaths and events in between. In fact, as one moves forward toward the mid- and later nineteenth century, the decline of specific religious meaning is evident in Pennsylvania German folk art generally. Even with regard to the once-religious form, "the *Taufschein* ultimately functioned more as a record of birth than as either a record of baptism or as a reminder of its meaning" (Weiser, *Fraktur*, p. 6). In the present exhibition, this recording emphasis is particularly evident in the aforementioned birth records made for John Bachman (fig. 20) and Lydia Glätz (fig. 21).

It needs to be pointed out in the discussion of "context" that *fraktur* documents did not in any sense attain the status of official church documents. *Fraktur* production grew out of customs by which some form of testimony and record was given for family purposes, associated with the role of the sponsors at the occasion of baptism. Perhaps the best description in Pennsylvania German studies is that provided by Pastor Weiser, who indicates that "baptismal *fraktur*" is to be related to the idea of gift giving at Baptism: "In European church life the sponsor ("godparent") of the child occupied a unique place in his life. One of the activities of the sponsor involved presenting a monetary gift on the day of baptism. And one of the forms of wrapper this gift acquired over the centuries was a hand-drawn greeting, a memorial of the event's meaning—a reminder of the need for faith and action consistent to it. These memorials came to have the child's name, the date of birth and baptism subjoined to them about the time of the Pennsylvania German immigration" (Weiser, *Fraktur*, p. 6). Some early Pennsylvania *fraktur* forms retain a sense of the solemnizing importance of witnesses at the church's administration of baptism. An important example in the collection of the Heritage Center is a *Geburts-und-Taufschein* (attributed to Wilhelm Antonius Faber) made in or after 1816 for Augustus Enck, "son of Johannes and Catharina Enck" (fig. 11). The piece is thoroughgoing in its attention to the details of ecclesiastical officiation and witness, indicating that baptism was administered (on Christmas day!) by "Rev. Faber, Reformed Preacher" and that "the baptismal witnesses (*Taufzeuger*) were Johannes Schiffler and his wife Catharina." Although *fraktur* documents of this sort were not commissioned by church or public authorities, they frequently contain as much information as any official certificate might supply. One *fraktur* scrivener, Johannes Spangenberg (before 1755–1814) uses the single term *Taufschein*, rather than *Geburts-und-Taufschein*, perhaps suggesting "that he found the baptism of the child more important than its human birth" (Fabian, p. 13).

Figure 8: Lewis Miller, "Interior of Old Lutheran Church in 1800, York, Pa.," circa 1820.
Lewis Miller (1796–1882) provides visual documentation in almost Dickensian detail of daily life. Of particular interest in this drawing is the prominence given to the choir as well as to paintings of religious subjects on the facade of the balcony of the church. (Courtesy of the York County Heritage Trust)

In Pennsylvania, although *fraktur* certificates were produced by scriveners for baptism of infant children, it must be kept in mind that such documents were by no means a requirement or expectation of ecclesiastical authorities. *Fraktur* documents were not housed in church archives but rather kept in the household, frequently folded and placed in Bibles or other religious books, or perhaps stored wherever space might be found in chests. Occasionally, *fraktur* birth-and-baptismal records were pasted onto the underside of the lid of the chest for safekeeping. One such example in the Heritage Center collection, attributed to the so-called Sussel-Washington artist, is a birth record for Maria Potzer, affixed to the underside of the lid of her dowry chest whose external decoration also contains her name painted on the front (illustrated in Earnest and Earnest, *Fraktur: Folk Art and Family*, p. 180).

While many *fraktur* practitioners were schoolmasters in the parochial schools of Pennsylvania, and thereby could be said to have worked in a context with affiliation or sponsorship by religious bodies, it would seem that few clergy were active scriveners and producers of *fraktur* documents. One interesting case was Daniel Schumacher, whose ordination was doubtful, but who nonetheless made efforts to impress upon *fraktur* recipients the idea that he was a bona fide Lutheran pastor. On a 1781 *Taufschein* made for Johan Henrich Rausch (illustrated in Weiser, *Fraktur*, p. 13) Schumacher has written, "And it is here corroborated and confirmed in pastoral faith by me Daniel Schumacher, p.h.t.," which Frederick Weiser indicates is a reference to the title of "Evangelical Lutheran Pastor in America in the Province of Pennsylvania in Weissenburg Township, the County of Northampton" (Weiser, *Fraktur*, pp. 12–13). Schumacher uses the explicit terms *Evangelisch Lutherisch Pfarrer* to define his ecclesiastical position. On a marriage record made by him for the betrothal of Daniel Bentzinger and Maria Weinmann he has again inscribed his credentials as Lutheran Pastor (fig. 14).

Another figure reputed to have held clergy status was Henry Young (1792–1861). E. Bryding Adams suggests that he may have been the "Mr. Jung" who applied for ordination at the Reformed Synod in the 1820s, but her claim is not substantiated.

It would seem that to pursue the idea of clergy *fraktur* artists as evidence of some official religious status of the art form will yield little fruit. *Fraktur* was produced rarely by clergy, and though it was frequently an activity of the rural schoolmaster, monetary incentives were readily apparent. Indeed, it has been pointed out that the widespread involvement of schoolteachers in this activity amounted to a kind of "*Taufschein* trade" (Weiser, "Ach wie ist die Welt so Toll!," p. 57). Some others examples, not necessarily bringing financial compensation, were the work of amateurs, often members or relatives of the family of the recipient.

Turning from the question of makers to that of recipients, the religious function of *fraktur* might be said to reside in the function of recording baptism, whether as infants in "church-type" denominations, or recording births and providing place for later documenting of baptism in other groups. Even the suggestion that the recording of births is no longer a religiously significant function might be tempered somewhat with the acknowledgment that the motive for preserving such information is grounded in the importance of the family and household as spiritual community, where work and daily activity are ordered toward religious purpose.

In the Pennsylvania German settlement of York County, Ontario, the use of the *Taufschein* had become so widespread among Mennonites that it was made even by Mennonite practitioners. Early schoolteachers in Markham Township were of Pennsylvania background, and very possibly of Lutheran or Reformed affiliation, and they used forms at home in those infant baptizing traditions, modifying their use for Mennonite recipients. What is interesting is that by mid-century, even an Ontario-born Mennonite scrivener such as Christian L. Hoover continued to use the "Lutheran/Reformed" type in his hand-drawn forms made for family and relatives in the 1850s.

The unconscious appropriation by one group of another's religious conventions has a long history, to be certain. In a very different context, it is notable that early Christians utilized Jewish rituals and customs, as well as conceptual and artistic expressions from Greece and Rome. In a reverse situation, a Jewish scholar had to remind adherents in the tenth century that a developing practice of orienting synagogues toward the East needed to be called into question because of it amounted to an inadvertent imitation of the Christian tradition, rather than the early Jewish view that such structures should face Jerusalem (DeBreffny, *The Synagogue*, p. 26) It is not surprising, then, that in rural Pennsylvania German settlements there should be an uncritical borrowing of practices, texts, and forms for use at a practical level, even when at a theoretical one they may seem inconsistent with theological tenets of one group or another.

The flexibility of these forms extended even beyond their simpler role in recording births. In at least one instance, a Pennsylvania *fraktur* artist amalgamated the functions of the *Taufschein* and the *Vorschrift*, a school-related document discussed separately. This seemingly unlikely combination is seen in a remarkable example in the collection of the Heritage Center of Lancaster (fig. 39). In this unusual specimen, the artist has brought together the recording aspects of documenting birth and baptism with the exhorting aspects of displaying spiritual reminders grounded in scriptural and devotional texts. Whether the reminder was effective is in doubt, of course, given the probability that within the household, a *Taufschein* was less likely to be displayed than stored.

Reflection

The Church as the place of entry into salvation and the school as the place of learning the basics of the moral/spiritual life this side of salvation provided meaningful religious contexts for two of the most significant forms of Pennsylvania German *fraktur*. It has been suggested that the *Taufschein* was far and away the most popular *fraktur* form, perpetuated from its earliest hand-drawn forms for more than a century by countless mass-produced versions by Pennsylvania printers. Its later usage lost much of its earlier church-rootedness, particularly as it became less a baptismal certificate and more a simple chronological record of birth, and it came to be used in sectarian contexts, where infant baptism was not practiced. The *Vorschrift* eventually died, particularly with the dissolution of the German-language parochial school, while the *Taufschein* continued a life greatly altered, watered-down, and largely out of touch with its religious roots. But for those important decades leading toward and past the end of the eighteenth century, these two forms expressed simply but elegantly much of religious life in communities of faith and places of moral instruction in the Pennsylvania German countryside.

Very little study has been given to the role of the parochial school in the folk life of the Pennsylvania Dutch. Its days were numbered when, in 1834, the Commonwealth passed a free-school act which empowered townships, upon vote, to create free schools within their jurisdiction. Although it would take three and a half decades for the last strictly parochial school to close, there is no question but that the 1830s were years of major change in Pennsylvania German life in other respects as well. An old institution—baptismal sponsorship—died out; not unrelated, confirmation became more important in church life than baptism. Industrialization eclipsed the small-town craftsman and the art that craftsman had often used totally un-self-consciously to make his product more salesworthy. While economic factors undoubtedly played important roles in these major revisions in Pennsylvania German life, the decline of the parochial school dare not be underestimated . . . (Weiser, "Fraktur," p. 230).

But in the second place, schoolmasters used *fraktur* even more directly to enhance their income. This was the most widespread use of *fraktur*. . . . Originally it consisted of drawing and penning in the significant data to a *Taufschein* (baptismal certificate). From the 1780s on, printed forms were available . . . (Weiser, "Fraktur," p. 231).

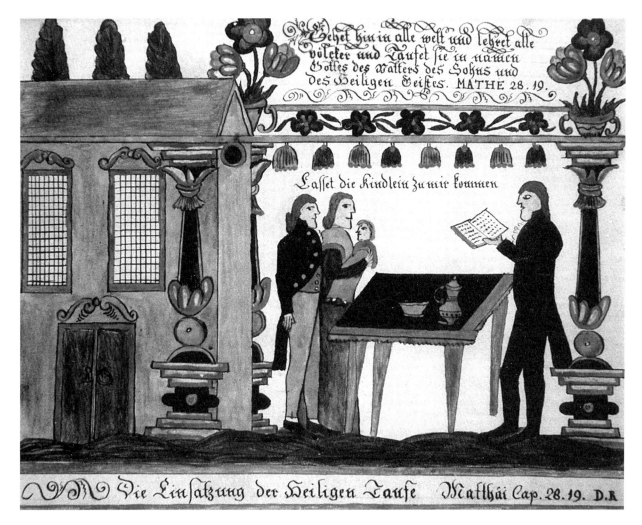

Figure 9: Durs Rudy. A baptism, circa 1825–1830.
Durs Rudy is exceptional in the degree of pictorial detail provided in his *fraktur*, including contemporary events in the life of the religious community. The occasion here is the baptism of an infant, at which the presiding clergyman reads the exhortation by Jesus in Matthew 28:19 to go into the world, teaching and baptizing, and including also the words, "Let the children come unto me." (Collection of Joan Johnson)

Figure 10: Ephrata Cloister Press. Birth-and-baptismal certificate, 1784.
An Ephrata Cloister printed form, with coloring-in by Johann Henrich Otto and lettered information added by Henrich Dulheuer. The form records dates of both birth and baptism of Jacob Weydmann, as well as name of the officiating pastor and witnesses for the baptism.
(Courtesy of the Heritage Center Museum of Lancaster County through the generosity of Mr. and Mrs. Richard Flanders Smith)

Figure 11: Wilhelm Antonius Faber. Birth-and-baptismal certificate, circa 1816. This work is entirely hand done, with cutout work as well as drawn and painted border decoration. Like the earlier printed Ephrata form, this document provides birth and baptismal information, along with a religious text reminding the newly baptized Augustus Enck that he has the gift of blessed life given by the suffering of Christ. (Courtesy of the Heritage Center Museum of Lancaster County through the generosity of Mr. and Mrs. Richard Flanders Smith)

Figure 12: Berks County artist. *Taufschein* for Anna Maria Dornbach, circa 1810 (20 cm. x 34 cm., 8.25" x 13.25").
Less common than records of birth and baptism are those which also provide information as to confirmation, here inscribed "and confirmed in her youth." (Courtesy of the Ungerbassler Collections, Phillips Museum of Art, Franklin and Marshall College)

Figure 13: Henry Dutye. *Taufschein* for Georg Wild, circa 1784. This elaborate *Taufschein* indicates the name of "Pastor Muhlenberg" (Henry Melchior Muhlenberg) and also the confirmation of Georg Wild by "Pastor Schultz in the evangelical Lutheran Christian faith." (Courtesy of the Winterhur Museum)

Figure 14: Daniel Schumacher. Marriage record, circa 1779. This very early marriage certificate records the marriage of the honorable Daniel Bentzinger and the youthful Maria Weinmann in 1770. At the bottom is lettered a "wedding text," based on Scriptures (Tobias: 7:15). (Collection of Richard S. and Rosemarie B. Machmer)

Figure 15: Andreas Kolb. Wedding wish, n.d. (24 cm. x 20.3 cm., 9.5" x 8"). Written as a "wish from a loyal friend," the text expresses exhortations to bride and bridegroom to remain faithful to God who "will put a crown on you in heaven as a gift of grace." Noteworthy here is the unusual degree of correlation of picture and text, with portraits of bridegroom and bride at center and heavenly crown above. (Courtesy of the Schwenkfelder Library and Heritage Center)

Figure 16: Henrich Otto and Henrich Dulheuer, *Taufschein*, 1784. By the late eighteenth century the design of printed *Taufscheine* had become formalized, with conventionalized border decoration surrounding standardized text and provision of blank spaces for infill of names and specific information. Documents such as this Ephrata printed form permitted the recording of the events of birth and baptism (note here the omission of the baptism date for Valentin Miller, who may have been a Mennonite and hence not baptized until young adulthood). (Collection of Dr. and Mrs. Donald M. Herr)

Figure 17: Joseph Lochbaum. *Taufschein* for Anna Maria Burkholder, circa 1830. Lochbaum, a well-traveled schoolmaster in Pennsylvania and Ontario, used the "Church"-type *Taufschein* in the Mennonite community in Markham Township, north of Toronto. More often than not, the updated information did not get added to the blank heart on the occasion of the recipient's baptism ten or more years after the birth date recorded on the form. (Courtesy of the Markham District Historical Museum)

Figure 18: Christian L. Hoover. *Taufschein* for Daniel Hoover, 1854. Working at a late date, Christian L. Hoover's hand-drawn records are adapted from earlier printed forms, as diverse as those by Henrich Dulheuer and Wilhelm Lepper, particularly evident in his rendering of birds as well as vines and flowers. (Private Collection)

Figure 19: Anonymous. *Taufschein* for Johannes Grov, 1807.
An unidentified artist whose work is found in both Pennsylvania and Ontario, this scrivener made by hand what had become a printed convention, with central text flanked by birds and floral decorations. (Private Collection)

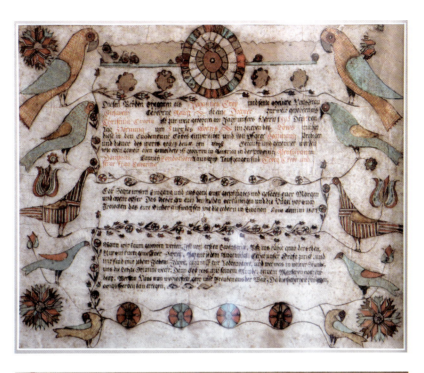

Figure 20: Signed by Eli Haverstick. Birth record for John Bachman, circa 1832.
The decline of explicitly religious functions of *fraktur*, noted by Frederick Weiser in his discussion of the Pennsylvania *Taufschein*, is evident here, where the function of witnessing baptism has given way to the simpler recording of date of birth. (Courtesy of the Heritage Center Museum of Lancaster County, given in memory of Elizabeth and Mortimer Newlin by V. P. Newlin and Lucy Bell Newlin Sellers)

Figure 21: Samuel Bentz. Birth record for Lÿdia Glätz, after 1811.

Similar in spirit to New England records of birth is the work attributed to Lancaster County schoolmaster Samuel Bentz (1792–1850). With no mention of baptism, its interest is less sacramental than geneaological. (Courtesy of the Heritage Center Museum of Lancaster County through the generosity of the James Hale Steinman Foundation)

Figure 22: Anonymous. Birth record for Sarah Strausbaugh, 1849.

A rare example of "Roman Catholic" *fraktur*, this simple hand-drawn composition records in English language the birth of Sarah Strausbaugh. Traditional Pennsylvania German folk art motifs such as birds and flowers are accompanied by the more explicitly ecclesiastical image of the cross. (Owned by June Lloyd)

Figure 23: Illuminated prayer book, 1844. Found in several Ontario-German households, these prayer books for home use complemented the Latin missal used in the Mass. They contain morning prayers, evening prayers, and prayers in various sections of the Mass, each accompanied by a hand-decorated page. Of interest is the combination of ecclesiastical symbols with generalized Germanic folk art motifs. (Courtesy of Dora Lewis, Rare Book Room, University of Waterloo)

Figure 24: Anonymous. Drawing, circa 1810
(16.6 cm. x 9.9 cm., 6.5" x 3.75").
This drawing and that following are unusual in their inclusion of "Byzantine" images of saints, likely borrowed from engraved versions, possibly those found on holy cards popular in Roman Catholic communities. This small specimen was very likely given to a studious pupil as a presentation *fraktur*. (Courtesy of the Rare Book Department, Free Library of Philadelphia, No. FLP 723)

Figure 25: Anonymous. Drawing, circa 1810 (22 cm. x 20 cm., 8.5" x 7.625").
Like the preceding example, an image derived from the tradition of the Byzantine icon is creatively amalgamated with more familiar Pennsylvania floral decoration, including the cross-legged angels found frequently as *Taufschein* border decoration and by John Adam Eyer to decorate songbooks and texts. (Collection of the American Folk Art Museum, New York; promised gift of Ralph Esmerian)

Figure 26: Deep Run Mennonite Schoolhouse, built 1842. Though built later than the prime period of German-language instruction and the making of *fraktur* by teachers for their pupils, this Bucks County stone schoolhouse is virtually unchanged in form from its predecessors. (Michael Bird Photo)

Figure 27: Christopher Dock. *Eine Einfältige und grundlich abgefaste Schul-Ordnung* (Germantown: Christoph Saur, 1750).
It has been suggested that many of Dock's pedagogical ideas set forth in his *Schul-Ordnung* found their way into Pennsylvania German parochial schools. His recommendation that diligent scholars should be rewarded with a drawing of a bird or flower may have been instrumental in the practice by which teacher/*fraktur* scriveners sometimes made presentation *frakturs* for their pupils.

Figure 28: Anonymous. *Vorschrift* for Barbara Meyer, 1848 (20 cm. x 31 cm., 8" x 12.25").

The didactic tone of the *Vorschrift* in this piece made for the young Barbara Meyer is expressed in its recommendation that diligence in youth is a necessary preparation for joy in eternity. (Courtesy of the Jordan Historical Museum of The Twenty)

Figure 29: Abraham Heebner. *Vorschrift*, 1772 (19.5 cm. x 2.3 cm., 7.75" x 9").
Taken directly from scripture, the text quotes Ecclesiastes 18:20–26 on the theme of preparing for judgment, being ready in the event that death should come unexpectedly. Its theme is that of repentance in "this time of sin" in anticipation of that later "time of wrath" (*dies irae*). (Courtesy of the Schwenkfelder Library and Heritage Center)

Figure 30: Isaac Z. Hunsicker. *Vorschrift*, 1830. Schoolmaster Isaac Hunsicker made several *Vorschriften* when he was a teacher at Lower Salford Township, Montgomery County, as in this example which speaks of anticipation of entry into the eternal kingdom of Heaven. A few years later he would move to Waterloo County, Ontario, where he continued to be active as a schoolmaster/*fraktur* artist. (Collection of Clyde and Ellen Herr)

Figure 31: Anonymous. Drawing of bird and tulip, early nineteenth century (11 cm. x 9 cm., 4.5" x 3.5").
Typical of "flower or bird" presentation *frakturs* made by teachers for pupils is this small drawing executed by a schoolmaster in the early nineteenth century at Vineland, Ontario. (Courtesy of the Canadian Harvest Collection, Joseph Schneider Haus Museum)

Figure 32: Combination *Vorschrift/Taufschein*. Multipurpose documents abound, as in the example of birth-and-baptismal records which include marriage information, but the combination of a *Vorschrift* and *Taufschein* is unusual. (Courtesy of the Heritage Center Museum of Lancaster County through the generosity of the James Hale Steinman Foundation)

Figure 33: Hans Jacob Brubacher. Lord's Prayer text, for Johannes Bähr, 1764 (5.6 cm. x 5.7 cm., 2.25" x 1.25"). The fascination with this prayer known by every child is evident in its appearance in many forms, including microscopic hand-lettered versions which were probably regarded as calligraphic challenges to scriveners. This early text is the work of Mennonite schoolmaster Hans Jacob Brubacher. (Courtesy of the Winterthur Museum)

Figure 34: Anonymous. Text, Apostles' Creed, circa 1820 (20.5 cm. x 33 cm., 8" x 13"). Though many *Vorschriften* and religious texts drew upon scriptures and emphasized ethical maxims, the occasional example reiterates articles of faith, in this case the Apostles' Creed. The document could have been made in a "Church" community (e.g., Lutheran or Reformed), but the Apostles' Creed was to be found in Mennonite prayer books as well. (Collection of Mennonite Historians of Eastern Pennsylvania)

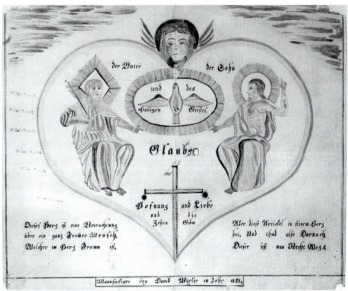

Figure 35: David Bixler. Text with Trinity, 1828 (31.5 cm. x 39 cm., 12.5" x 15.75"). *Fraktur* texts with a doctrinal basis are comparatively rare. This example makes reference to the Trinity, and also of the importance of tenets of faith: "This heart is a meditation upon a perfectly pious man who has the articles [of the Creed] in his heart."(Courtesy of the Rare Book Department, Free Library of Philadelphia, No. FLP 66)

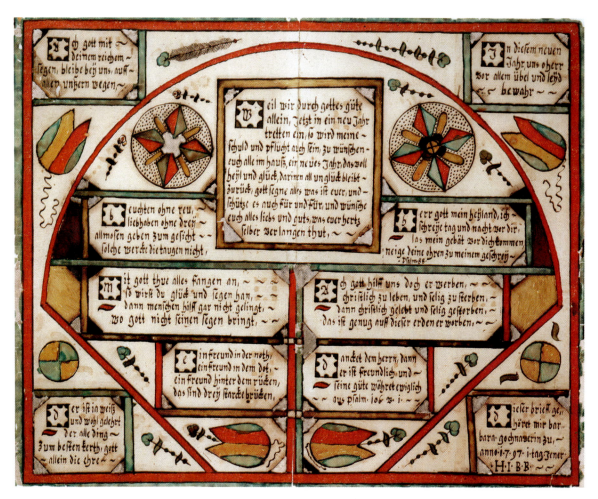

Figure 36: Hans Jacob Brubacher. New Year's greeting, 1797 (30.2 cm. x 38.3 cm., 12" x 15") This artist, who frequently signed his name HIBB, made several New Year's greetings in the late eighteenth century. The text recognizes God's goodness in permitting us to enter into the New Year, and asks that the Lord provide protection and blessings in the days ahead. (Courtesy of the Rare Book Department, Free Library of Philadelphia, No. FLP 1060)

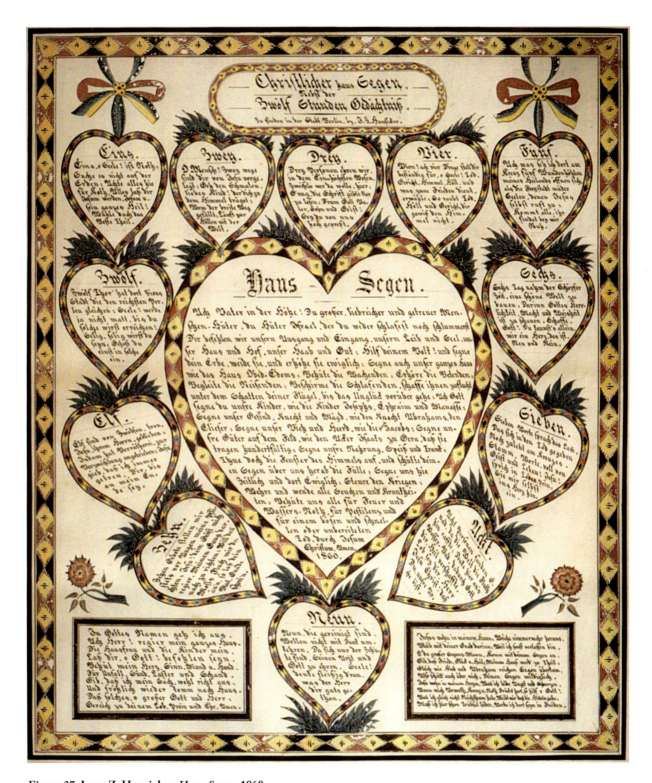

Figure 37: Isaac Z. Hunsicker. *Haus-Segen*, 1860.
Hunsicker executed this hand-drawn copy late in his life from an earlier printed form from Augsburg in Germany. Texts enclosed within hearts meditate upon symbolic aspects of the twelve hours and wish God's blessings on all who come and go. (Courtesy of the Canadian Harvest Collection, Joseph Schneider Haus Museum)

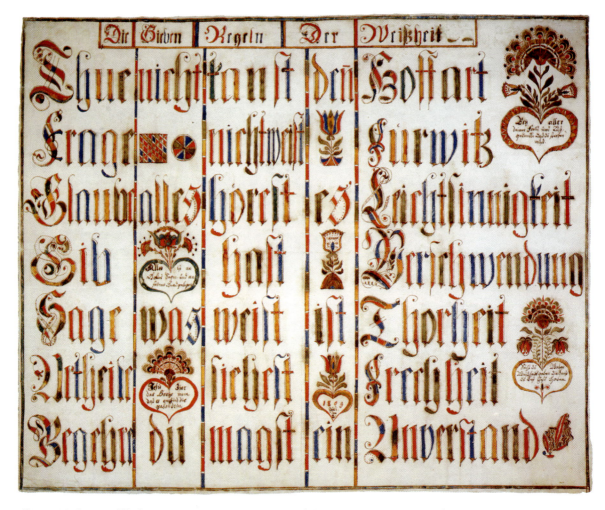

Figure 38: Susanna Heebner. *Seven Rules of Wisdom*, 1809 (35 cm. x 48 cm., 13.75" x 19"). A didactic piece popular in Schwenkfelder circles, Susanna Heebner's text reflects upon "Seven Rules of Wisdom." The form is that of a puzzle, in which one must read the text in "right" order, beginning each rule with a word in the left column. One then reads the second column downward, and selects the word in the third column directly across from that in the first. The process is repeated for columns four and five. (Courtesy of the Schwenkfelder Library and Heritage Center)

Figure 39: Isaac Z. Hunsicker. *Mensch Lebe Fromm und Gut*, 1861.
Using the device of a zoomorphic alphabet, in which letters are comprised of animal and plant forms, the maxim is short and direct: *Live well and devoutly*. (Courtesy of the Canadian Harvest Collection, Joseph Schneider Haus Museum)

Figure 40: Durs Rudy. Religious metamorphic puzzle, 1832 (16 cm. x 10 cm., 6.25" x 4").
The metamorphic puzzle book, with turn-up pages, was a popular didactic device in New England, where its religious message paralleled the primer used widely in schools. This Pennsylvania-German version emphasizes the theological motifs of the Fall (images of Adam and Eve), Redemption (the Crucifixion of Christ), and the urgency of reflecting upon life's choices in the face of inevitable mortality. (Courtesy of Lehigh County Historical Society)

Figure 41: Anonymous. Quote from Ecclesiastes, "All is Vanity," circa 1790 (13 cm. x 8 cm., 5" x 3"). An ever-present reminder that the true prize lies beyond. As far as the present world is concerned, we need only to turn to the words of Ecclesiastes: "All is vanity." (Private Collection)

Figure 42: Regina Krauss. Text/*Golden ABC*, 1815 (192 cm. x 32.2 cm., 7.5" x 12.75"). With each letter representing a key word in the message, the text is strongly sermonic, advocating a life of love of Jesus in response to Christ's supreme act of love in shedding his blood for sinners. (Courtesy of the Schwenkfelder Library and Heritage Center)

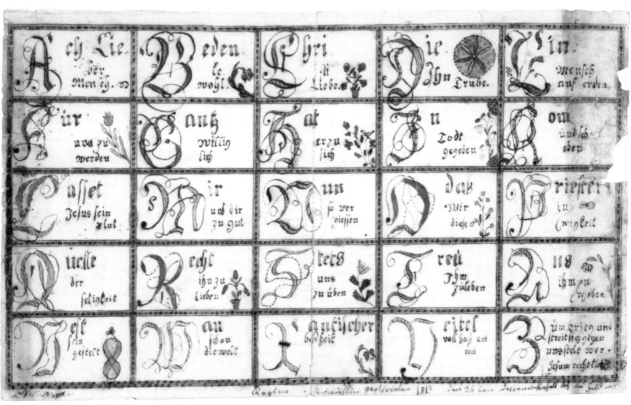

Of the many books espousing Pietistic theology, it was works by Arndt and Tersteegen which were especially popular in Pennsylvania German households. Many are the examples of *fraktur* which quote lines from these sources.

Figure 44A *(top left)*: Gerhard Tersteegen, *Geistliches Blumen-Gaertlein Inniger Seelen* (Germantown: C. Sauer, 1747)

Figure 44B *(top right)*: Johann Arndt, *Vom Wahren Christentum* (Benjamin Franklin and Johann Boehm, 1854.

Figure 44C *(left)*: Johann Arndt, *Paradies-Gärtlein* (JSH copy—the book was still popular in Canada in the late nineteenth century).

(Courtesy of Special Collections, Franklin and Marshall College)

CHAPTER II

THE WIDE SWEEP OF PIETISM: PENNSYLVANIA GERMAN RELIGION WITHOUT BORDERS

ACROSS DENOMINATIONAL LINES: PIETISTIC THEMES IN FRAKTUR

*Das Hertze
Mein soll jesu
gantz ergaben seÿn*

*Jesus Wohn in meinem
Hertzen wann ich
leide angst und schmertzen*

*This heart of mine shall be
completely given to Jesus*

*Jesus dwell in my heart
when I suffer anxiety and pain*

These words, framed within hearts at the bottom of a text written in 1783 by schoolmaster John Adam Eyer for his pupil Angenes Landes, could be said to epitomize the direction in which religion had turned in late-eighteenth century Pennsylvania German culture. Eyer, a Lutheran, and his pupil, most likely a Mennonite, have ancestral roots in traditions which, although different from one another, were equally rich in doctrine or confession, each with its social structure and collective sense as spiritual communities. The words here, and for that matter most of the fuller text, reflect a different spirit—highly individualized, personalized, and internalized. Missing are the great collective themes of creed or social ethic. Here the outlook is subjective, psychological, and interpersonal. Even the larger central text of Eyer's *fraktur* composition focuses less on Christ as King in Heaven and more on Jesus as friend on earth.

To consider this shift of emphasis in *fraktur* texts, it is important to consider what was being read or heard or simply kept on the shelf in the German-speaking religious communities of Pennsylvania at the end of the eighteenth and in the early nineteenth century. While most households had a copy of the Bible and sometimes later editions of various religious books from the sixteenth century, the increasingly popular religious publications from the mid-eighteenth century and later reflected a more Pietistic emphasis with little connection to earlier Reformation themes.

While Pietism as a religious movement was originally a development within Lutheranism in the seventeenth and eighteenth centuries, emphasizing personal transformation and subjective feeling, in part a reaction against hardening Protestant dogmatism, the phenomenon spread beyond Lutheran borders to make its impact among other religious groups as well. Drawing upon the teaching and writing of Philipp Jakob Spener (1635–1705) and August Hermann Francke (1663–1727), Pietism transcended previously defined Protestant denominational boundaries. In Pennsylvania, its spread meant the gaining of popular acceptance within German Reformed, Mennonite, and Moravian followings, and even within the confines of the Ephrata community. Decidedly Pietist writings such as Johann Arndt's *Vom Wahren Christentum* were soon to be found in households within each of these communities. Among principal tenets of Pietism were the idea of religion as a return to the heart ("heart religion"), the balancing of justification with sanctification, and emphasis upon *Wiedergeburt* ("rebirth"). Indeed, Stoeffler goes so far as to say that "Pietism's cornerstone was the doctrine of rebirth" (Stoeffler, *Continental Pietism*, p. 72).

Many are the Pietistic texts which describe the journey from sin to salvation, and the long struggle (*Busskampf*) with sin and leading to "conversion." The personalism of Pietistic spirituality led to emphasis upon Jesus as one with whom the believer seeks friendship. The longing (*Sehnsucht*) for unity with Jesus is a recurring theme in hymn and *fraktur* texts, as it was in such important devotional works as Arndt's *Vom Wahren Christentum*, his *Paradies-Gärtlein*, or Gerhard Tersteegen's *Geistliches Blumen-Gaertlein Inniger Seelen*. These themes are tightly bound together in the hymn "Mein Gott, das herz ich bringe dir" found in various editions of the Lancaster Conference hymnbooks, the *Liedersammlung* and *Unpartheyische Gesangbuch:*

Figure 45: Anonymous. Religious text, late eighteenth century (17.9 cm.. x 22.8 cm., 7" x 9").
Fraktur texts and also hymn verses repeatedly espoused the Pietistic assessment of the world as a place of strife and a vale of tears. The text announces, "There is nothing but distress, quarrel, fear and agony. . . . We people are driven from paradise and have great sadness here in the content of this world. . . ." (Courtesy of the Schwenkfelder Library and Heritage Center)

Figure 46: Maria Heebner. Text, 1843 (18.8 cm. x 33.7 cm., 7.5" x 13.25").
The lament in Ecclesiastes regarding the vanity of the present world had experienced a revival in the Pietistic judgment of earthly life. Maria Heebner's text instructs the believer to "avoid pleasure for the eye, vile joy, luxury, as well as filth and mud. . . ." (Courtesy of the Schwenkfelder Library and Heritage Center)

My God! This heart, I bring to Thee
A present and a gift;
For you're requesting this from me;
I'm mindful, now, of this.

Give me your heart, my child, you say,
I love it 'tis much worth.
You'll not find rest another way
In heaven, nor on earth.

And thou, dear Father, take it then,
My heart do not despise
I'm giving it as best I can,
Unto me, turn Thy face.

Be gone, world, sin; for I present
My heart to Christ alone.
Receive this gift, a commitment,
Keep it Lord, for Thy own.
(translation in Stoltzfuss, pp. 49–50).

In *Fraktur* this sentiment is found in endless examples as the popular phrase *Mein Herz ist Dein allein*, or, similarly:

Geb Jesu dein Herz
dies ein ist Noth

Passages in this hymn and many others like it in *fraktur* witness to the Pietistic belief that faith and works, justification and sanctification, are inextricably linked together, as do the forgiveness of sin and the establishment of a new person. This Pietistic emphasis upon transformation, rooted in the writings of Spener has been described as a "Johannine and Pauline metaphor . . . a completion and enhancing of the equally biblical juridical metaphor of justification" (Brown, p. 67).

The "inwardness" of Pietism is a prominent theme in the work of Arndt, who suggested the importance of daily reminders to oneself of its importance: "A Christian should turn away at least once a day from all outward things and enter into the ground of his own heart" (*Vom Wahren Christentum*, p. 821 [quoted in Stoeffler, p. 101]).

With its inward orientation, Pietistic spirituality frequently expresses a disdain for the world, as the way of the flesh, and a vale of tears. This outlook is found variously on texts by an anonymous artist , by Abraham Kriebel (1782), Maria Heebner (1843), and Ontario's Anna Weber (1879) (figs. 112 and 119). All bear witness to the world as a place of temptation, sin, and confinement:

Strive that your enthusiasm glows,
and that your first love draws you
away from the world. . . .

Take your soul with fear,
your salvation with trembling;
Here in this body's hell
you are suspended in danger daily.
(Abraham Kriebel, 1782)

Figure 47: Abraham Kriebel. Religious text, 1782 (33.6 cm. x 20.6 cm., 13.75" x 8").
Copied from hymn lines in the *Neu-Eingerichtetes Gesang-Buch*, Abraham Kriebel's text urges the believer to a life of "striving"—striving for the gate, striving for Christ and rejecting Satan, striving for the eternal life and ignoring the vanities of earthly existence. Heavy indeed is the Pietistic judgment of the world as a vale of tears. (Courtesy of the Schwenkfelder Library and Heritage Center)

> *There is nothing but vanity....*
> *Plague, lament, trouble and quarrel,*
> *grief, sorrow, fear and misery....*
> (Maria Heebner, 1843)

That Pietistic themes reached across the borders of denominational religion and were carried from Pennsylvania to Canada can be seen in the woeful view of the world as a vale of tears expressed in a Schwenkfelder text from the late eighteenth century and a Mennonite text by Ontario's Anna Weber written in the late nineteenth century:

> *There is nothing but distress, quarrel,*
> *fear and agony in this vale of tears.*
> (Anon. Schwenkfelder artist, late eighteenth century)

> *Finally it is necessary to take leave*
> *of this evil world.*
> (Anna Weber, 1879)

In contrast to the harshness of the external world is the warmth, even described as a sweetness, of an inner religiosity, what Stoeffler has referred to as "heart religion." Frequently the language is that of home and homelessness. Whereas the world is an alien place, from which the soul seeks to depart in order to find its true home in Jesus. A notable example attributed to the "Ehre Vater artist" is illustrated in Frederick Weiser's study of small presentation *frakturs* (*The Gift Is Small, The Love is Great*, p. 97). Here, a juxtaposed snake and heart (intimations of competing prizes—the snares of the world or the heart of Jesus?) are accompanied by the words:

> *Remind yourself, my treasure dear,*
> *Of him who loves you with good cheer....*
> *How sweet his life would one day be*
> *If he could say you belong to me.*

This relational concept of belonging to Jesus appears in almost endless variation in many examples of Pennsylvania *fraktur*, notably in bookplates, in presentation *frakturs*, and also in the corners of larger texts (figs. 3 and 51):

> *This heart of mine shall belong*
> *to you alone, O Jesus!*
> *Glory to God on high.*
> (Andreas Schultz, his *Catechism*, 1786)

> *Give Jesus your heart*
> *in joy and pain, in life and Death*
> *This one thing is necessary.*
> (John Adam Eyer, title page of music book for Maria Gross, 1788)

The pervasiveness of Pietistic sentiment is evident in the popularity of texts by a Lutheran schoolmaster/*fraktur* artist such as Eyer, producing texts for pupils, many of whom were Mennonite, and appearing in the *fraktur* of Ephrata and among the Schwenkfelders. A "Sweet Jesus" text penned by Eyer in 1783 (fig. 53) refers to Jesus as one "who makes my heart merry," and promises that "with Him comfort may always be found...." Similarly, the Mennonite scrivener Hans Jacob Brubacher was to compose a text for Susanna Gochnaur (fig. 48) with an arrangement of hand-drawn hearts and the words, in what constitutes an ultimate expression of domestic Jesus imagery:

Oh my dear heart, little Jesus,
makes for you a pure and soft bed,
calling you to rest in my heart,
that I may never again forget you."
(Hans Jacob Brubacher, New Year's Greeting, 1797)

In some texts, the transcendent image of Christ in Heaven seems to have given way completely to a more companionable depiction of Jesus on earth, one who comforts and befriends the lonely soul in distress. In a religious text whose composition resembles closely the design conventions of Eyer, the Mennonite schoolmaster Huppert Cassel (b. 1751) printed a heart-enclosed text in 1807 (fig. 52) which, in effect, combines the traditional hymn of praise to the sacred name of Jesus with the more Pietistic theme of personal friendship: "Jesus my friend, my honor and glory, treasure and wealth of my heart. I cannot show sufficiently how highly your name can delight."

In these diverse lines from hymns and *fraktur* texts the subjective, personal "heart religion" of Pietism reached across confessional borders, making its appeal to Pennsylvania German religionists of every Protestant faith community. *Sehnsucht* as an expression of spiritual longing leaps forward from the pages of Ephrata hymnbooks, and equally from the hymns and *fraktur* of Moravians, Lutherans, Reformed, Mennonites, and Schwenkfelders. Assessment of its weaknesses and strengths is varied, from Martin Marty's view that Pietism constituted in moral terms a "Christian retreat from responsibility as it has been viewed in the past" (Brown, p. 12) to the positive view by Donald Bloesch that Pietism was one of the "wellsprings of new life in the church" (*Ibid.*, p. 12). What is clear is that Pietism, with its emphasis upon conversion, repentance, sanctification, yearning for a home beyond the misery of this world, and personal communion "in the heart" with the divine manifest in Jesus, spoke meaningfully to many individuals who were not always attracted to the formal orthodoxy of established Protestant churches in German and Pennsylvania.

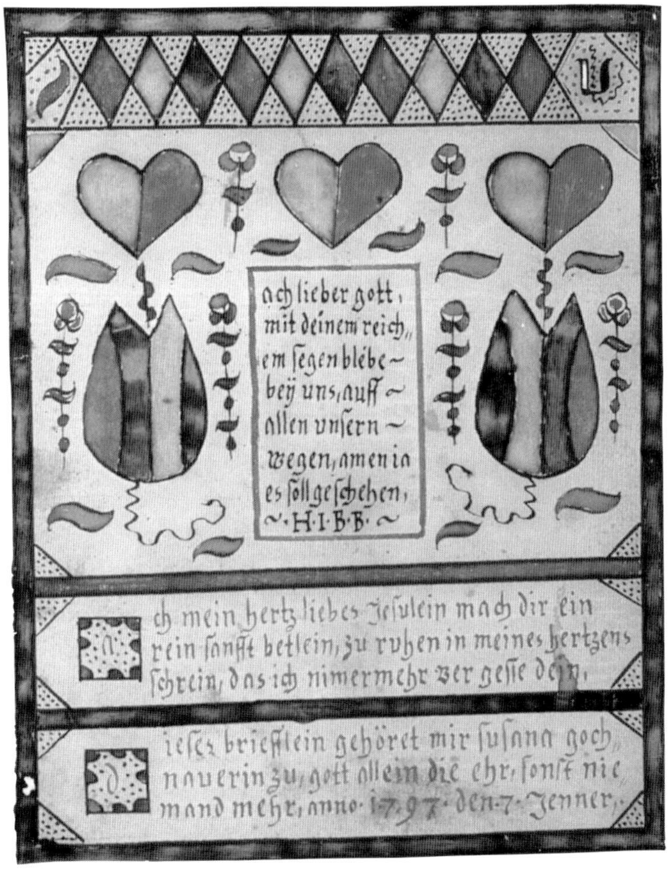

Figure 48: Hans Jacob Brubacher.
New Year's greeting, 1797.
Although references to the heart abound in other contexts, Pietistic theology found the image particularly congenial in its emphasis upon emotional and inner spirituality. It appears here in one of the several New Year's greetings drawn by Mennonite scrivener Hans Jacob Brubacher. (Collection of Clarke E. Hess)

Figure 49: Attributed to David Kriebel. Drawing, 1804 (9.8 cm. x 16.9 cm., 4" x 6.75").
One of the most oft-repeated *fraktur* texts—"This heart of mine shall be yours alone O Jesus." (Courtesy of the Schwenkfelder Library and Heritage Center)

Figure 50: "Ehre Vater" artist. Text, circa 1800 (16 cm. x 14 cm., 6.25" x 5.50").
Whether the subject is divine or human love is left ambiguous in this Pennsylvania presentation *fraktur*, with images of snake and heart suggesting competing objects of devotion. (Collection of H. Richard Dietrich Jr., Philadelphia; photo by Will Brown)

Figure 51: John Adam Eyer. Songbook for Maria Gross, 1788 (10 cm. x 16.5 cm., 4" x 6.75") Another ubiquitous *fraktur* text, especially popular on illuminated songbooks: "Give Jesus your heart in joy and pain, this one thing is necessary." (Courtesy of the Jordan Historical Museum of The Twenty)

Figure 52: Huppert Cassel. Text, 1807 (20 cm. x 16.4 cm., 8" x 6.5").
Heart imagery as companionship with Jesus: "Delight in Jesus, my friend." Frequently there is to be seen a correlation of content and form with the device of a heart used to frame the text. (Courtesy of the Schwenkfelder Library and Heritage Center)

Figure 53: John Adam Eyer. Religious text, 1783 (21.7 cm. x 18 cm., 8.5" x 7").
The Lutheran schoolmaster Eyer draws deeply from the well of Pietism: "Jesus is in my heart." (Courtesy of the Schwenkfelder Library and Heritage Center)

Figure 54: Anonymous. Painted chest, early nineteenth century (63 cm. x 127 cm. x 54 cm., 24.75" x 50" x 17.75").
A rare occurrence in the decoration of furniture is this depiction of figures of Adam and Eve, most likely borrowed from a printed *fraktur* version of the subject. (Courtesy of the Winterthur Museum)

CHAPTER III

REPRESENTATIONAL ART:

PICTORIAL IMAGERY

IN FRAKTUR

To the degree that early *fraktur* in Pennsylvania was comprised primarily of texts with illuminated margins or interstices, early embellishments tended to be stylized and decorative, rather than natural and pictorial. Ephrata illuminations fall into somewhat of a special category with their depictions of angels and human figures, sometimes in connection with the content of texts. Even so, much of Ephrata illumination consists of stylized paired birds, hearts, tulips, and other floral motifs. When we move away from Cloister manuscripts and begin to survey the immense range of *fraktur* texts and drawings in the divergent faith communities of the Pennsylvania German countryside, we find a preponderance of conventionalized motifs drawn in changing combinations, but almost always derived from a small inventory of stylized designs and compositions. Pictorial representation of human subjects is a rarity, and virtually the entire output can be assigned to a handful of artists. Notable among these are Friedrich Krebs, Henry Young, Arnold Puwelle, and Durs Rudy. An exceptional case is Ludwig Denig, whose Picture-Bible, possibly a unique example in America, is the subject of a major study by Donald Yoder, *The Picture-Bible of Ludwig Denig, A Pennsylvania German Emblem Book.*

Within the category of *fraktur* which might be termed *pictorial*, certain subjects appear more frequently than others. The reasons for the particular selectivity of Pennsylvania German pictorial subjects may be more practical than philosophical, having to do in large part with the matter of readily available printed sources from which artists copied or adapted their hand-drawn versions.

Pictorial *fraktur* examples do include a wide range of subjects when account is taken of single or exceptional expressions. In this case the diversity of religious subjects treated includes images of the Holy Family, the Nativity of Jesus, Jesus preaching to his disciples, and a few others. Notably absent are the Last Supper, the *Pieta*, and other subjects which had long been popular in historical Christian artistic depictions.

A second category, however, is comprised of subjects which were depicted on more frequent occasion and by several rather than one artist. To say that these images were common would be misleading, to be certain, but their apparent similarity to engraved images in books, broadsides, and birth/baptismal records suggests their general acceptability to a Pennsylvania German audience. Two themes in particular were illustrated by various *fraktur* artists, notably (a) the temptation and fall of Adam and Eve, and (b) the Crucifixion of Jesus. The two themes have, of course, an intrinsic connection, in that they are the events which bracket the fall and salvation of humankind, the destructive sin of humanity, and the saving grace of God. A third theme treated primarily by one or two artists but on repeated occasions is that of the Prodigal Son. This story is woven into the same fabric as the other two events, becoming in its journey imagery the prototypal message of loss and recovery, estrangement and reconciliation, fall and redemption.

Adam and Eve

Pennsylvania printers who produced images of Adam and Eve were numerous. Among them were Henrich Otto, C. A. Bruckman, Heinrich Sage, and others. In some cases the immediacy of inspiration for *fraktur* artists is dramatically evident. There is little doubt, for example, that the schoolmaster Gottlieb Saur—an example of his work appears in Michael S. Bird's *Ontario Fraktur* (fig. 101); a similar example is illustrated in Weiser and Heaney's *The Pennsylvania German Fraktur of the Free Library of Philadelphia* (fig. 216)—made a direct copy of the form printed only slightly earlier by Heinrich Sage in Reading. Likewise, Ontario-born Joseph D. Bauman appears to have copied an early nineteenth-century printed form by J. Bauman of Ephrata in the hand-drawn Adam-and-Eve pictures which he drew in the 1880s (fig. 66). Durs Rudy, an unusual *fraktur* artist in view of his frequent pictorial depictions of religious subjects, may have seen German printed sources which found their way to Pennsylvania. Sometimes artists combined traditional subject matter with everyday details associated with Pennsylvania agrarian life. In a work by an anonymous practitioner, Adam and Eve are surrounded with animals more at home on the modern farm than in the biblical garden (fig. 63). In this respect he was in keeping with early German artists such as Albrecht Dürer who repeatedly recast scriptural stories in Franconian topographical and architectural contexts.

Figure 55: Photograph. Iron stoveplate, Adam and Eve, 1745. The subject of the Fall had a very early appearance in Pennsylvania decorative arts as a motif on cast-iron stoveplates. This example from 1745 was photographed by Henry C. Mercer, and appears as Plate No. 88 in his publication, *The Bible in Iron*. (Courtesy of the Mercer Museum, Doylestown, Pennsylvania)

In other instances, however, artists worked in a style which seems to owe little to printed sources, even though the subject matter was no doubt recalled from such contexts. Martin Gottschall's treatment of Adam and Eve (fig. 60) is almost expressionistic in its free-handed use of color and line. Even details of the story of the temptation sometimes undergo modification, embellishment, or addition. It is interesting in this regard to take note of Joseph D. Bauman's drawing and the printed version which seemingly served as his reference. In these and several other *fraktur* treatments, a second apple is being plucked by Eve from the tree already as the first is being handed to Adam! The general similarity of images to printed and textual traditions probably insured the acceptability of this popular image, even to those who were inclined toward inventory counts.

A more literal rendition without Bauman's inflationary embellishments is a Durs Rudy treatment (fig. 63) in which Eve reaches for one apple while Adam reaches forward in ready anticipation, shifting emphasis from the tradition which depicts Eve as the seductress and Adam as hapless victim. Indeed, the text used by Rudy casts its blame directly upon the serpent: *Adam und Eva im Paradeis werden von der Schlangen verfürt.*

Figure 56: Abraham Heebner. Adam and Eve, 1830 (25.5 cm. x 19.8 cm., 10" x 7.75"). Mortality is the theme of the text accompanying this representation of Adam and Eve. Scarcely had Eve enjoyed the sweet taste of the fruit when "death came at the same hour." (Courtesy of the Schwenkfelder Library and Heritage Center)

Figure 57: Maria Heebner. Adam and Eve, 1843 (25.7 cm. x 19.9 cm., 10" x 7.75").
These two virtually identical works by brother and sister may in fact be hand-colored tracings taken from a printed original. (Courtesy of the Schwenkfelder Library and Heritage Center)

What were the functions of various Adam-and-Eve images printed or drawn by hand in nineteenth-century Pennsylvania, found principally in *fraktur*, but occasionally also on cast-iron stoveplates (fig. 55) or even a painted chest in the Winterthur Museum collection (fig. 54)? Were they ever anything more than decorative accents, or were the settings indicative of some religious or moral purpose?

In some instances, the image of Adam and Eve is drawn or printed in immediate proximity to the biblical or extrabiblical texts recounting the story of the Fall and its consequences for humanity. Joseph D. Bauman's hand-drawn version is accompanied by a hymn text in the form a fictional re-creation of a conversation between God and Adam and Eve (fig. 66). This broadside and printed forms from which it is derived suggest a domestic purpose, since by definition broadsides were "posted" and hence served as visual reminders of the themes which they proclaim by word and image.

But not all Adam and Eve images appear in broadside form. Several examples are included as details on other documents, notably birth and baptismal certificates. Here they appear as decorative elements flanking a central text. By dividing the figures of Adam and Eve, *fraktur* artists could resort to the same familiar symmetry which characterized the placement of floral and other more abstract ornamentation attached to texts of many kinds. A notable example is the position of these figures on either side of a record of birth and baptism for Catharina Maÿer done after 1787 in Frederick County, Maryland (illustrated in Weiser, *Fraktur*, p. 41). A similar situation can be seen with a Friedrich Speyer *Taufschein* (fig. 61).

Allowing for the possibility that artists simply lifted convenient artistic details from handy sources and inserted them willy-nilly into or beside any text at hand, there does remain nonetheless the interesting possibility that on occasion someone might have thought that the Adam and Eve story is relevant to the fact of birth and the event of baptism, themselves understood in the theological tradition as moments of entry into fallen humanity (birth) and admission to saved or potentially savable humanity (baptism). These works are connected in paradoxical manner, of course, in that the first parents were born into innocence which they lost through human sin, whereas the child whose name is here recorded is born into sin which is overcome through divine intervention manifested in baptism. In such contexts the association of image and religious function is plausible, whether or not the intention is overt.

Figure 58: Anonymous. Adam and Eve, early nineteenth century (20 cm. x 14.9 cm., 8" x 6"). An "updated" treatment of the subject, with modern farm animals! The practice of including local subjects in religious scenes has an honorable German ancestry in sixteenth-century engravings by Albrecht Dürer and others. The text reads: "The tree of knowledge of good and evil: First Book of Moses" (Genesis 2:17). (Courtesy of the Schwenkfelder Library and Heritage Center)

Figure 61: Friedrich Speyer. *Taufschein*, circa 1874.
As with many printed versions, this printed *Taufschein* makes reference to that early identify of birth and mortality, when the newborn child finds itself already thrown into the world of sin and death. The point is given visual reinforcement in the Speyer imagery of Adam and Eve committing the first sin whose immediate consequence was death. (Collection of Dr. and Mrs. Donald M. Herr)

Figure 59 *(opposite page, top)*: Attributed to Martin Gottschall.
Adam and Eve, circa 1830 (19.5 cm. x 32.2 cm., 7.50" x 12.75").
A highly abstracted treatment, the artist places Adam and Eve in an arcaded central panel flanking a stylized floral motif rather than the familiar tree with fruit and serpent. (Courtesy of the Rare Book Department, Free Library of Philadelphia, No. FLP 1036)

Figure 60 *(opposite page, bottom)*: Attributed to Martin Gottschall.
Adam and Eve, circa 1830.
The artist was at his expressionistic best when he turned to the subject of Adam and Eve standing by, almost awaiting the provocative next step by the serpent. Placing the Tree of Knowledge on a terraced mound calls to mind medieval folkloric connections between Eden and Golgotha, where the cross of Christ is said to have been made from the tree in the Garden and was set up on the same mound. (Collection of Joan Johnson)

Figure 62: Friedrich Krebs. Double *Taufschein*/marriage certificate, circa 1800. Even as the newly married young couple Christian Steltz and Catharina Schmidt were celebrating the joys of beginning life together, the marriage certificate made for them by Friedrich Krebs reminds them of the sin of humankind's first parents. (Courtesy of the Abby Aldrich Rockefeller Folk Art Museum, Williamsburg, Virginia)

Figure 63: Durs Rudy. Drawing of Adam and Eve, circa 1825–40 (19.7 cm. x 24.4 cm., 7.50" x 9.50").
In a manner similar to other artists, Durs Rudy accompanies the visual image with an "explanatory" description, "Adam and Eve were led astray by the serpent." (Courtesy of the Winterthur Museum)

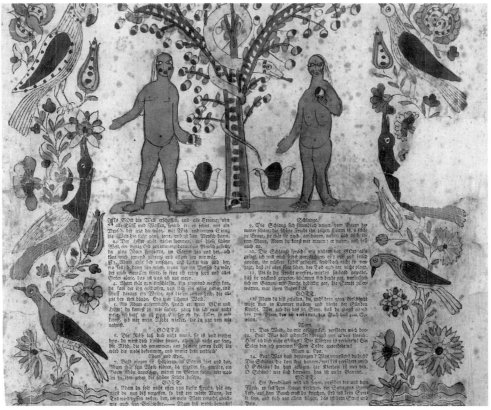

Figure 64: Friedrich Krebs. Decoration on printed broadside, circa 1800 (33.8 cm. x 40 cm., 12.875" x 15.75").
The text recounts the story of God's creation of the world and of its special inhabitants, Adam and Eve, whose act of disobedience brought on the consequences of strife, pain, and death. (Courtesy of the Titus C. Geesey Collection, Philadelphia Museum of Art)

Figure 65: Anonymous. Adam and Eve, circa 1805.
The image of Adam and Eve found its way into many households through the printed versions produced at various presses throughout southeastern Pennsylvania. This hand-drawn version, probably adapted from such printed sources, includes angels used by John Adam Eyer and others. (Collection of H. Richard Dietrich Jr.)

Figure 66: Joseph D. Bauman. Adam and Eve, circa 1880. In the late nineteenth century Ontario-born fraktur artist Joseph D. Bauman had a local printer prepare several copies of a hymn text, leaving space in which he inserted his hand-drawn picture of Adam and Eve. His work is derived from printed sources such as a J. Bauman version published at Ephrata in the early nineteenth century. (Courtesy of the Canadian Harvest Collection, Joseph Schneider Haus Museum)

Figure 67: Anonymous. *Taufschein* for George Manger, 1809 (12.625" x 15.50"). Birth as entry into the world of sin and death is made apparent in the inclusion of the story of Adam and Eve as border decoration of this *Taufschein*. The text in the right-hand heart rejoices nonetheless in the fact that baptism enables the believer to contemplate the blessings of eternity. (Courtesy of the Abby Aldrich Rockefeller Folk Art Museum, Williamsburg, Virginia)

Prodigal Son

The artist Friedrich Krebs seems to have been particularly attracted to the story of the Prodigal Son as a *fraktur* subject, having done several sets of drawings which taken together provide an unfolding narrative of events. Krebs seems to have found inspiration for his drawings in an astonishing variety of sources—German folk tales, Grimm fairytales, engravings, heraldry, and Scripture.

Friedrich Krebs (1749–1815) was a Lutheran schoolmaster in Dauphin and other counties. He was a prolific artist who for a fee produced birth-and-baptismal certificates (printed forms which he customized by addition of his hand-drawn tulips, birds, and other ornamental details) for various families in the regions where he lived. He also decorated broadsides whose texts served as spiritual reminders of virtue and attention to the divine purpose of all live and work. In addition, he is known for a large group of drawings based on well-known biblical stories. The story of the Prodigal Son who abandons and then, much humbled by the world's experiences, returns to his all-patient and forgiving father, was a favorite subject for Krebs. In the manner of early narrative-style Christian art, recalling perhaps Giotto's chronological treatment of

the story of the parents of the Virgin Mary, Krebs gives us a sequential account of the central episodes in the Prodigal Son's journey. The piece here is comprised of installments, a series of vignettes, showing the Prodigal Son leaving the comfort of his father's home, his traveling and succumbing to the world's temptations, his state of despair as he stands shoeless and forlorn among swine, and finally his return and joy at the welcome given to him by his father.

An interesting choice of scene is depicted by an unknown artist, with its portrayal of the Prodigal Son reveling in the company of prostitutes (fig. 71). The artist here pauses to bring to our attention the delights and pleasures of the wayward actions of the Prodigal Son, rather than moving quickly to the judgmental imagery of his downward slip into desolation and despair. Still, we understand the tragic consequences of his debauchery and the transient nature of temporary pleasure which only briefly disguises the reality of his loneliness and anguish. The sense of being lost, that important stage preceding the experience of forgiveness and redemption, is echoed in *fraktur* texts such as that done by Durs Rudy (fig. 68) who drew upon Psalm 102, in which the lonely soul calls out, "Hear my prayer, O Lord, and let my cry come unto you. . . ."

The Prodigal Son story was as popular in rural Pennsylvania as perhaps it had been more than three centuries earlier in the rural German countryside in which Albrecht Dürer illustrated this famous journey of wayward humanity. Dürer placed these events in the familiar countryside setting of Franconian barns and peasant dress, and Krebs established a Pennsylvania context by the placement of tulips and other popular folk art motifs in borders and margins of his text and drawings. In these diverse cultures, the story con-

Figure 68: Durs Rudy. Text, circa 1805. The theme of being lost in the wilderness is the subject of this elegantly lettered text by Durs Rudy. The source is Psalm 102:1–2: "Hear my prayer, O Lord, and let my cry come unto Thee. Hide not Thy face from me in my need. . . ." (Collection of Paul Flack)

Figure 69: Durs Rudy. Prodigal Son (four scenes), 1830.
The story of the Prodigal Son exemplifies the ancient tale of selfish action, repentance, and return. The narrative sums up in compact form the Christian theological understanding of Fall and Salvation. As in other pictures, Durs Rudy dresses his biblical characters in clothing styles of the late eighteenth or early nineteenth century. Unexpectedly, the narrative begins in the lower right corner, moving clockwise to the return of the reunion of father and son at upper right. (Collection of Joan Johnson)

stituted both a practical enjoiner from father to son on the virtue of practicing thriftiness and also an earthy visual theology of the primordial story of Adam's fall from grace. It did more, though, by compressing the long stories of Adam and Christ, Fall and Salvation, Sin and Forgiveness. In its few short episodes, the Prodigal Son story traced the full circle from the theme of empty wandering and abandonment to purposive pilgrimage toward fulfillment and reconciliation with a steadfast and all-loving God. The connection is made explicit here by inclusion of the biblical text, "Father, I have sinned in heaven before you" (Luke 15:11–32). When all is said and finished, this is a much-loved telling of the ultimately fulfilling story of the triumph of divine love over human weakness.

Figures 70A, 70B, 70C, 70D: Friedrich Krebs. Prodigal Son, early nineteenth century (each 21 cm. x 33 cm.. 8.50" x 13.25").

Krebs depicted this subject on several occasions, giving us a multipaneled narrative of the biblical story. The son is shown leaving his father, falling into a life of reckless indulgence, experiencing the punishments of loneliness and despair, and then returning home to be welcomed by his ever-faithful father. (Courtesy of the State Museum of Pennsylvania, Pennsylvania Historical and Museum Commission)

Figure 71: Anonymous. Prodigal Son reveling among harlots, late eighteenth century (15 cm. x 17 cm., 5.75" x 7").
The biblical story of the Prodigal Son's wanderings include an account of his reveling among harlots. The artist here dresses the son smartly and the women tartly—evoking perhaps a nineteenth-century sense of the evils of the tavern and public house as portrayed in sermonizing of the day. (Courtesy of the Abby Aldrich Rockefeller Folk Art Museum, Williamsburg, Virginia)

Crucifixion of Jesus

On more than one historical occasion, the fact of Jesus' Crucifixion has been cause for hesitation as a subject for artistic depiction. While early Christian artists drew or painted many religious themes familiar today, the Crucifixion was not one of them. Images of such familiar topics as the Last Supper, the Good Shepherd, the Baptism of Jesus, or of various miracles are to be found painted on the walls of an early Christian baptistery at Duro-Europas near the Euphrates or in the Roman catacombs from the early third century, the Crucifixion as an artistic representation appears no earlier than the fifth century, and then only rarely. Various theories as to this omission include a purported hesitancy on the part of the fledgling Christian church to emphasize unduly the death Jesus at the same time that early preaching and writing was focused upon the authority and redemptive power of Christ in Heaven.

In America, the rarity of the Crucifixion in Pennsylvania German folk art would hardly grow out of the same reasons as those of the early Church, but is perhaps more clearly related to the relative scarcity of religious pictorial imagery in *fraktur* per se. The subject does appear in a handful of late printed forms, notably by C. F. Egelmann, Johannes Armbrust, and D. May, whereas, by contrast, Adam and Eve are the subject of more than

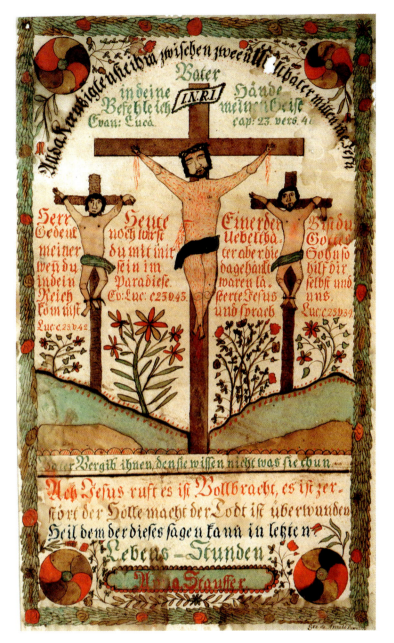

fifty printed versions. In each case, the Crucifixion appears not as a single subject but rather as one of a group of illustrations accompanying birth and baptismal texts.

The number of hand-drawn representations of the Crucifixion is modest, indeed, and can be seen to be the work of a still smaller group of artists. One of these, Arnold Puwelle (1809–1879), is reputed to have been a Roman Catholic adherent. If so, he would have undoubtedly been highly familiar with pictorial religious art, seen in church interiors, illustrated Massbooks, holy cards, and religious pictures commonly hung in Catholic households. Several examples attributable to his hand (fig. 72) bear stylistic resemblances to one another. An additional artist who treated this subject on more than one occasion is Durs Rudy (cf. fig. 74) whose denominational affiliation was most likely Lutheran or Reformed. In either case, he functioned within religious traditions in which representational art could be seen in some churches as well as in engraved images in Bibles and devotional books.

Another scrivener who was attracted to the Crucifixion as a *fraktur* subject was Friedrich Krebs (1749–1815). He produced an elaborate version which belongs to the Landis Valley Farm Museum (fig. 76). That Krebs was aware of engraved images of the Crucifixion is readily apparent. He is known not only for his primitive calligraphy and drawings, but even for his fascination with collage, in which he pasted together his own hand-drawn work with printed matter. An

Figure 72: Arnold Puwelle. Crucifixion and text, circa 1840 (32.5 cm. x 20.5 cm., 12.5" x 8"). Several drawings of the Crucifixion rendered between 1847 and 1853 by Arnold Puwelle (1809–1879) cite scriptural passages which accompany the traditional portrayal of Jesus hung between two thieves. It seems likely that Puwelle had seen engraved images of this subject, from which he drew inspiration in his two-dimensional, simplified treatment. His visual representation is accompanied by scriptural citations from the twenty-third chapter of Luke. The text at bottom of this piece made for Maria Stauffer reminds the believer of the saving call of Jesus which can be heard even at the hour of death. (Courtesy of the Rare Book Department, Free Library of Philadelphia, No. FLP 310)

interesting example is shown in Klaus Stopp's multivolume study of printed certificates, *The Printed Birth and Baptismal Records of the German Americans* (vol. 1, p. 78), whereby Krebs pasted onto his own work several scenes cut out from imported German brocade paper. This piece is particular revealing in that it indicates the fact that some Pennsylvania artists were familiar with European engravings in addition to the many forms printed in the Commonwealth.

At what date does the Crucifixion or Cross first appear in Pennsylvania German *fraktur*? Possibly the earliest appearance of the plain cross in Pennsylvania *fraktur* dates from 1747, if not slightly earlier. It occurs as a decorative design in a music book manuscript hand-drawn by an anonymous artist. The designs, texts, and notes were included in two collections of hymns, the *Zionitischer Weyrauchs Hügel* and *Das Gesäng der einsamen und verlassenen Turtel-Taube* (cf. Weiser and Heaney's *Pennsylvania German Fraktur of the Free Library of Pennsylvania*, fig. 22). The latter was published by the Ephrata printing press in 1747. This early image, in contrast to the pictorial character of the Crucifixion, is in this instance confined to the spare simplicity of the geometry of intersecting lines, and is in fact subordinated to the status of a decorative detail within a larger composition of an enclosing heart, flowers, and paired birds.

The earliest-known hand-drawn representation of the Crucifixion itself may date from 1786, with the anonymous publication of what might be called a liturgical broadside (illustrated in Weiser and Heaney's *Pennsylvania German Fraktur*, fig. 219). Printed in southeastern Pennsylvania, possibly Lancaster, this form is comprised of a text leading the reader through the church year, and accompanying hand-rendered pictures serve to illustrate the various occasions, including Christmas, New Year's Day, Epiphany, Lent, Maundy Thursday, Good Friday, Easter, Ascension Day, Pentecost Sunday, and Trinity Sunday. Good Friday is illustrated by a drawing of Christ crucified between two thieves. Together the text and images serve as a basis for reflection on the meaning of the death and Resurrection of Jesus, with the concluding reminder that against the redemptive power of the Resurrection death has no ultimate power.

In the interplay between printed and drawn images, it is not always clear as to who was copying whom, but the similarity of engraved images to earlier examples in the German-speaking states in Europe suggests that *fraktur* artists would have had access to numerous printed versions. In Lutheran and Reformed Churches, painted panels or hung pictures could also have been influential, as has been suggested by Don Yoder in his *Picture-Bible of Ludwig Denig* (p. 16). Mention has already been made of Lewis Miller's picture of the interior of the "Old Lutheran Church" in York, in which religious scenes are prominently painted on the panels of the balcony. While the number of printed or hand-drawn *fraktur* images of the Crucifixion is small, it would seem that after the appearance of a hand-drawn Crucifixion, ca. 1810, with accompanying text from Isaiah 42:1 referring to the "suffering servant" (illustration in Weiser/Heaney, fig. 218) there was a small outpouring of such representations largely from the 1820s through the early 1850s. Johannes Armbrust and D. May produced engraved versions of the Crucifixion around 1820 and 1840 respectively. The two artists whose names can be clearly associated with this subject, Durs Rudy and Arnold Puwelle, were active in the 1830s and 1850s. Several Puwelle examples are dated between 1847 and 1853. Another drawing of this subject, executed by Henry Young, is dated 1847 (fig. 75). Yet another rendering, in a rare context for Pennsylvania examples, is that drawn by Ludwig Denig as part of the extensive array of illuminations in his Picture-Bible, dated 1784. This early work precedes the Armbrust printed forms by four decades, and the liturgical broadside with its text and hand-drawn images by two years. But it does not precede yet other engraved images such as those found in illustrated Bibles, emblem books, and various devotional manuals for the Protestant home. Yoder argues, "by the eighteenth century, framed engravings of Adam and Eve in the Garden of Eden, Noah's Ark, the Prodigal Son, the Crucifixion and other

Figure 73: Anonymous. Crucifixion and text, circa 1810 (32.4 cm. x 21.4 cm., 13.5" x 8.5").
Similar in form to engraved holy cards popular in Roman Catholic communities, this drawing by an unidentified artist is underscored by a text from Isaiah 42, and the formulaic expression, "the cross is His lot, He wins the salvation of the pious." (Courtesy of the Rare Book Department, Free Library of Philadelphia, No. FLP 1031)

Figure 74: Durs Rudy. Crucifixion (Matthew 15:34), circa 1825–30.
Durs Rudy drew multiple versions of the Crucifixion. In this example he amalgamates several scenes, including the Crucifixion, entombment, a modern church and other buildings, and a host of persons not usually grouped in the same scene: Mary, Mary Magdalene, Joseph, and Salome. The soldiers wear uniforms more likely seen at the Battle of Waterloo. (Collection of Joan Johnson)

Figure 75: Henry Young. Marriage record for Johannes Kiess, 1847.

In this drawing, which dominates the brief text indicating its function as a marriage record for Johannes Kiess and Maria Marquand, Henry Young presents a traditional picture of the Crucifixion. Mary prays to one side, while on the other, the Roman soldier pierces the side of Jesus. The association of picture and text seem particularly accidental in this example, providing a cautionary reminder that one should not always expect consistency in analyzing the content of *fraktur* compositions. (Courtesy of the Titus C. Geesey Collection, Philadelphia Museum of Art)

Figure 76: Friedrich Krebs. Crucifixion of Christ (32 cm. x 39 cm., 12.75" x 15.50").

Very much of a "Church" image, this detailed *fraktur* by Friedrich Krebs is derived from engraved sacramental images in which the blood of Christ flows into the Eucharistic chalice. (Courtesy of the Landis Valley Farm Museum, Pennsylvania Historical and Museum Commission)

Figure 77: Anonymous. Drawing of Crucifixion of Christ, 1847 (34 cm. x 27 cm., 13.50" x 10.75").

Similar to other examples by this artist, Jesus is placed between two thieves, with accompanying scriptural texts indicative of human choice on the road to salvation—repentance or recalcitrance. To the repentant thief, Jesus speaks the consoling words, "Today you will be with me in Paradise." (Courtesy of the Abby Aldrich Rockefeller Folk Art Museum, Williamsburg, Virginia)

Old and New Testament subjects appeared on Protestant walls. . . ." (Yoder, p. 5), and elsewhere he observes that painted biblical scenes might have been displayed in various churches, not only Roman Catholic as one might expect, but Protestant as well, as in the case of Christ Lutheran Church in York.

An interesting piece of evidence, highly revelatory of how *fraktur* scriveners knew of European printed images of religious subjects, is to be seen in the earlier-mentioned example shown in Stopp (vol. 1, p. 78). Here, the *fraktur* artist Friedrich Krebs produced a collage of hand-drawn and engraved images in a *Taufschein* for Philip Schäfer done circa 1800. On other occasions Krebs had cut details from printed forms and stamped these on his hand-drawn certificates. In this case, his tastes were more extravagant—he cut up not ordinary paper but expensive brocade sheets imported from Germany by Thomas Dundas in Reading, Pennsylvania, and then affixed these to either side of the text he had written by hand. These brocade pieces consist of four biblical scenes, one of which is the Crucifixion. Another drawing of the Crucifixion between thieves in the collection of the Pennsylvania Farm Museum of Landis Valley (Landis Valley Associates, plate 48) probably by Durs Rudy, suggests a distant connection with the engraved image in the treatment of the radiant nimbus over the head of Christ, although in most other respects the primitive drawing owes little to the high style of the former. Like other examples by Rudy, the figures standing beneath the cross are identified by name and wear modern dress.

The pictorial representation of religious events was but a grace note in the long melodic line of Pennsylvania German *fraktur* imagery. It shares with the wider range of *fraktur* expression, however, the awareness of diverse sources of inspiration from paintings and engraved images. While some *fraktur* artists made more direct borrowings of pictorial subject matter, most practitioners made ongoing use of stylized motifs possessing only an indirect relationship to formal sources, expressed in parallel manifestations in the decorative embellishment of Pennsylvania German furniture, ceramics, and textiles.

Figure 78: John Adam Eyer. Religous text, 1783 (20 cm. x 16 cm., 8" x 6.25").
The medieval theme of Christ as mystical bridegroom appears frequently in Pennsylvania German hymnody and *fraktur*. Quoting hymns from *Das Kleine Davidische Psalterspiel*, Eyer's text emphasizes the theme of the soul anticipating the wedding banquet: "I will love and do my utmost to please my bridegroom. . . ." (Courtesy of the Schwenkfelder Library and Heritage Center)

CHAPTER IV

BEHOLD THE MAN: THE MANY CHARACTERIZATIONS OF JESUS

One Lord, Many Faces

Many are the descriptions of Jesus found in *fraktur* texts as well as in Pennsylvania hymn collections and prayer books. The presence of many images—some seemingly contradictory—is sometimes taken by some interpreters as a weakness in historical/theological development. To others, such diversity may in fact be fully consistent with diversity in the earliest church community, already experiencing the conflicting cultural influences of Hebraic and Hellenistic worlds. In a modern context regarding images of Jesus in differing world cultures, it has been written: "The multiplicity of new images of Jesus is often attributed to and blamed upon the overly enthusiastic response of Asian and Latin American and African theologians. But what is overlooked is that this proliferation of images is not due only to the vigorous and passionate response of Asian Christians and others engaged in contextual Christologies, but is due also to the nature of the gospel narratives themselves, which lend themselves to a variety of expositions (Butler, p. 259).

Within the infinitely smaller geographic expanse of southeastern Pennsylvania, characterizations of Jesus, especially textual descriptions, are likewise remarkably diverse. Despite a relative paucity of images in visual picture form, textual images abound. In some respects, the situation is not entirely unlike that of the early church, where visual images were few but literary language abundant and variable. Perhaps texts had to supply what was not available by way of visual record. Indeed, Irenaeus, Bishop of Lyons, wrote, "the physical features of Jesus are unknown to us," and Augustine wrote in the third century, "we are completely ignorant of what He [Jesus] looked like" (Jobe, p. 14). It is interesting that the absence of pictorial documentation is given as a reason for the rise of symbolic imagery: "During the first two centuries of the Church's life, symbolic figures alone were used . . . what the incarnate Jesus really looked like was of interest neither to artist nor theologian (Jobe, p. 14).

Writers of hymns and scriveners of *fraktur* texts described Jesus as teacher, leader, friend, wounded savior, Second Adam, and mystical bridegroom. Visual symbols of Jesus are equally evocative in their diverse images of dove, plant, lamb, suffering servant, and pelican pecking its breast.

While familiar images of Jesus—such as those of Jesus as lamb or dove—have a long history and even a biblical background, some of the references in texts are of later origin, drawn frequently from later medieval symbolism or mystical imagery. While scholars differ as to how large an intentional role symbolism played in the consciousness of Pennsylvania German folk artists, recipients, and the population at large, all recognize the perpetuation of ancient language and imagery in texts and folk art, however unthinking or rote the repetition of familiar expressions and images may be.

Recurring Images of Jesus in Pennsylvania German Fraktur

Sweet Jesus, Friend

From the lofty imagery of Jesus enthroned in majesty in Heaven to intimate descriptions of Jesus as companion walking at one's side, *fraktur* texts speak in many voices indeed. Similar description variations abound in another text form, that of hymns found in various denominational collections and frequently known in several communities at once. An interesting case in point is the emerging imagery by the late eighteenth century in the songbooks used widely in parochial schools of eastern Pennsylvania, many of which were inscribed and decorated by prominent *fraktur* artists such as John Adam Eyer and others.

In her study of illuminated Pennsylvania songbooks, Suzanne Gross makes the observation that the hymns in these booklets provide evidence of a conceptual change regarding forms of Jesus imagery expressed. In particular, she notes that by the later eighteenth century, "The bitter [suffering] Christ of the Anabaptists gave way to the sweet, personal Christ of the Pietists (Gross, *Hymnody*, p. 88).

The personal relationship of believer with Jesus is found frequently in the *Notenbüchlein* done by various teachers in eastern Pennsylvania, and even in examples known to have been made for Mennonite recipients, it is Pietistic rather than specifically Mennonite themes which prevail (Gross, *Hymnody*, p. 213). The words of tender endearment, befitting a friend of long standing, are far removed from the words of "bitter death" in *Jesu meines Leben's Leben* in a later section of this discussion, especially when expressed so personally in a Schwenkfelder *fraktur* text:

Come dear friend of the soul,
the most beloved which my heart imagines;

A thousand times I desire you
for nothing else delights me....

Jesus, I call you my only pleasure.

These lines in a *fraktur* text made for Isaac Heebner (fig. 87) are taken from various sources, among them the heavily Pietistic German Baptist Brethren hymnal *Das Kleine Davidische Psalterspiel,* published two decades earlier.

Similarly, an 1807 religious text attributed to Mennonite schoolmaster Huppert Cassel (fig. 52), who made several *fraktur* specimens for Mennonite children, is unashamedly casual in its manner of addressing Jesus as friend: "Jesus my friend, my honor and glory, treasure and wealth of my heart." So intimate had Pietistic theology become that Jesus, who on a 1773 *Vorschrift* in the collection of the Free Library of Philadelphia (illustrated in Weiser/Heaney I, fig. 249) and a similar example in the Schwenkfelder Historical Library (illustrated in Moyer, fig. 5-67) is described in abstract terms as *Das wahrhaftige Licht* ("True Light"), could also be understood in personal terms as *Jesu mein Freund*.

Figure 79: Anonymous. Love letter, 1786 (20.2 cm. x 33.2 cm., 8" x 13").

Combining textual and pictorial images of hearts, this *fraktur* composition describes Jesus as "my chosen friend, my heart's bridegroom." So personal was Pietistic spirituality that a text directed to Jesus could take the form of a love letter: *Treue Liebe vereiniget unsre Hertzen* ("true love unites our hearts"). (Courtesy of the Schwenkfelder Library and Heritage Center)

Figure 80: Anonymous. *Vorschrift*, late eighteenth century.
The symbolic language of scriptural poetry from Ecclesiastes may or may not have been taken to heart by recipients, but even as merely a writing exercise, its words are poignant: "Arise my love, my fair one, and come away; For lo, the winter is past. . . . And the voice of the turtledove is heard in our land." (Courtesy of the Ungerbassler Collections of the Phillips Museum of Art, Franklin and Marshall College)

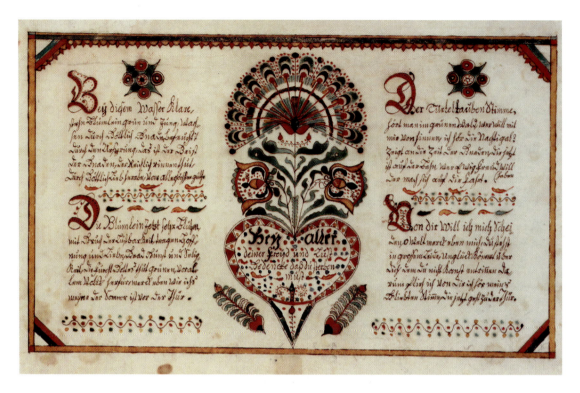

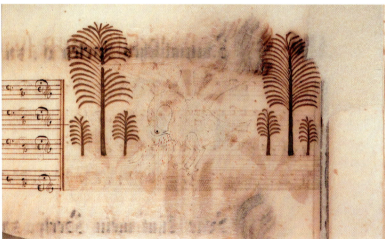

Figure 82: Anonymous. Illuminated page in *Das Gesang der einsamen und verlassenen Turtel-Taube*, 1747 (22.3 cm. x 17 cm., 8.5" x 6.5").
An ancient motif taken from non-Christian sources, notably various editions of the *Physiologus*, the theme of the pelican pecking its breast came to be understood as a symbol of Jesus shedding His blood for the salvation of humanity. (Courtesy of the Rare Book Department, Free Library of Philadelphia, No. FLP 1148)

Figure 81: Susanna Heebner. Text for Susanna Heebner, 1811 (20.8 cm. x 34 cm., 8.25" x 13.50").
A scriptural allusion received indirectly from hymnody, the text quotes verses of the *Neu-Eingerichtetes Gesang-Buch*: "One hears the voice of the turtledove in the green woods. . . . I hear the voice of my beloved which now goes to the door." Even if not taken religiously by its reader, the text's spiritual implications are securely grounded in the religious context of the hymnbook. (Courtesy of the Schwenkfelder Library and Heritage Center)

While the description of Jesus as friend emphasized the personal qualities of feeling, other imagery focused on the intellectual dimension, emphasizing Jesus not so much as friend as teacher.

Jesus as Teacher and Light to the World

In a rare pictorial representation of a scene from the public life of Jesus, *fraktur* artist Durs Rudy has chosen to emphasize his role as teacher. Quoting Matthew 28:18–19, Rudy presents Jesus invoking his divine mandate ("all authority in heaven and on earth has been given to me," and exhorting his disciples to undertake their teaching tasks to the world: "Go therefore and make disciples of all nations" (fig. 88). A hilly landscape with flowers below suggests the world into which Jesus' followers must go, while angels above allude to the heavenly source of the words he preaches. His placement on a pedestal on the highest ground makes evident his authoritative role as teacher and as God made flesh on earth.

Bringing the theme of Jesus' teaching into everyday life, a bookplate for Maria Clemer reminds her as a pupil and believer that "Christ's teaching shows me the way I shall go" (fig. 89).

Closely related to the concept of teacher is the notion of Jesus as Light to the World, particularly in terms of the Johannine image of light as the truth which overcomes darkness. A *Vorschrift* attributed to the Hereford Township artist (fig. 84) is an exercise in scripture copying, its text taken directly from the first chapter of the Gospel of John, in which Jesus is described in Hellenistic language as "the true light that came into this world. . . ." Another *Vorschrift*, dated 1773 (Free Library of Philadelphia: FLP1113) combines two very different images—Jesus as Light of the World and Jesus as Suffering Savior—with surprising cohesiveness. The connection made between the two images is that of light, the radiance which burst forth at the birth of Jesus and that which paled with the death of Jesus, when "the sun withdrew its light."

Second Adam

With repeated theological emphasis upon the consequences of that original sin which left humanity in an alienated state of separation from the object of its true spiritual desire, it is not surprising that an occasional *fraktur* text would focus its attention on an image capable of reversing that dark history. Relatively few are *fraktur* references to images of Jesus as "Second Adam" derived from I Corinthians 15:21–22, but a notable example (fig. 91) formulates the radically new prospect in almost-Anselmian words which present Jesus as God's chosen go-between or arbitrator who can negotiate humanity's re-entry into union with its divine source:

> *What Adam has spoiled, Christ won back.*
> *Whoever requests heavenly gifts can have them.*
> *Select my heart what is good for you,*
> *on whom your heart may rest. . . .*
> *He leads you to life.*
> *My highest good shall be God alone*
> *in Christ, my mediator. . . .*

The range of images is diverse, reflecting the varied influences of many sources—Scripture, early creedal formulations, Lutheran or Anabaptist Reformation theologies, medieval mysticism, Pietistic personalism and inwardness, and—frequently—randomly assembled fragments of unevenly mixed textual backgrounds combined within single *fraktur* compositions. In this respect, *fraktur* compositions are like hymnbooks—they gather together many theological resources from which believers may draw inspiration. They are not usually creative so much as reflective, serving to reinforce spiritual insights already received and accepted by those who might sing or read their texts.

Mystical Bridegroom

Alongside more familiar biblical images, the colorful references to Jesus as "bridegroom" were undoubtedly inspired by medieval symbolism and mystical writing on the image. To be sure, there are earlier roots for such "bride-mysticism" in the Church Fathers, notably St. John Chrysostom (circa 347–407), but the theme served more as an accent rather than a central motif until the Middle Ages when it was popularized by Bernard of Clairvaux (1090–1153) and others. Conrad Beissel was strongly attracted to this imagery, even to the point of creating a sisterhood at Ephrata based on the marriage theme with Christ Jesus as the Bridegroom of the Order (Ernst, p. 171). John Joseph Stoudt wrote extensively in what has become a most controversial interpretive work, *Pennsylvania German Folk Art: An Interpretation* (revised and adapted from his earlier *Consider the Lilies, How They Grow*), on the symbolism of the bridegroom, and has been criticized by some for broadening the symbolism too far as though it defined an essential strand of Pennsylvania German piety.

Perhaps the most significant resource for bridegroom imagery in Pennsylvania German culture is to be found in the writings of Johann Arndt (1555–1621). In his widely circulated *True Christianity (Vom Wahren Christentum)*, Arndt denounced the cold logic of theological disputation, calling intellectual treatises "useless" and "unnecessary." The real purpose of theology should be not so much abstract knowledge as personal renewal, specifically "renewal in Christ." Arndt's consistent theme throughout *Vom Wahren Christentum* is that personal renewal in Christ is "the purpose of all theology and the whole of Christianity. . . ." (*True Christianity*, p. 276):

This is the union with God, the marriage
with our heavenly Bridegroom, Jesus Christ,
the living faith, the new birth, Christ's
dwelling in us (Ibid., p. 277).

While the symbol of Jesus as mystical bridegroom pervaded much of Ephrata music and texts printed there, it had its place in the hymnody of other groups, as well. It appears in the Lutheran hymnody of Johan Walther, as well as in numerous Mennonite hymns in the various editions of the *Liedersammlung* and the Lancaster Conference hymnbook *Unpartheyisches Gesangbuch*. It can also be found in Schwenkfelder *fraktur* texts (fig. 79), where the image of bridegroom is mixed with that of Jesus as Lamb of God. The symbol was also utilized by schoolmaster John Adam Eyer in 1783 when he executed a *fraktur* text (fig. 78) which included the following verses:

I will love and do my utmost to please
my bridegroom in everything now. . . .

I will love and do my utmost my entire life
to adapt and to decorate myself with the
white wedding-garment, so that I may appear
with the pure at the wedding-joy of the Lamb.

Turtledove

The image of the dove, long associated in Trinitarian symbolism with the Holy Spirit, has also a connection with Jesus, particularly in its form as a turtledove. Because turtledoves are popularly understood as lovebirds, and depicted in verse and image in pairs, the connection with the bridegroom is a close one, since in both cases there is a reflection upon the theme of the poles of separation and unity in a love relationship. The turtledove is a central image in Ephrata songs and devotional writings as well as in visual folk art, where it sometimes appears in margins adjacent to references in texts. Indeed, *Die Turtel Taube* is in fact the name of the great Ephrata hymnal of 1747, and references to the symbol occur in many early Ephrata publications. Its full title, *Das Gesäng der einsamen und verlassenen Turtel-Taube Nemlich der Christliche Kirche,* indicates that the turtledove is equated with the Christian church on earth, as it seeks to be reunited with its partner in Heaven. The image is firmly rooted in scriptures:

My beloved spoke, and said unto me, Rise up my love,
my fair one, and come away; for lo, the winter is past,
the rain is over and gone, the flowers appear on the earth;
the time of the singing of the birds is come,
and the voice of the turtle [dove] is heard in our land
(*Song of Songs* 2:10-12)

References to the turtledove occur in diverse *fraktur* contexts, among them a *Vorschrift* in the collection of Franklin and Marshall College which quotes the *Song of Songs* passage literally (fig. 80). Another example, made in the Schwenkfelder community for Susanna Heebner in 1811 begins with the reference to the passing of winter and arrival of growing things in the summer: ". . . summer is at the door"—then proceeds to the central imagery: "One hears the voice of the turtledove in the green woods . . ." and then makes the final equation with the divine voice calling from beyond: "I hear the voice of my beloved which now goes to the door" (fig. 81).

Pelican Feeding Its Young (Jesus and Sacrificial Love)

The picture of the pelican pecking its breast, drawing forth its own blood to feed its young, is an ancient symbol associated with the doctrine of Christ's vicarious sacrifice on the Cross to redeem fallen humanity. The image occurs from time to time in Pennsylvania German *fraktur*, and textual references to Jesus' death as sacrificial intervention to save humankind is found in many *fraktur* texts. Like many hand-drawn motifs, this image was in all likelihood taken from printed sources, honoring the age-old Pennsylvania German practice of copying again and again.

An indirect source for this *fraktur* motif may be one outside of Christian symbolism per se, drawing indirectly from the ancient Greek or Latin *Physiologus*, an encyclopedic description of animals, birds, fish, and even stones, compiled for didactic purposes. The various chapters serve to illustrate points of Christian doctrine and morality, presenting descriptions of nature as allegorical references to deeper meanings. Among examples which were to become popular in Christian imagery are the lion, pelican, owl, unicorn, turtledove, and stag. All of these images appear in *fraktur*, as well as in other decorative arts. While the origins of *Physiologus* are elusive, there is general consensus that the earliest Christian treatise must have been written at Alexandria in the third century. Following the earliest Greek versions of *Physiologus*, there came Latin translations in the fourth cen-

Figure 83: Anonymous. Pelican drawing, early nineteenth century (10 cm. x 6.5 cm., 4" x 1.75"). A small drawing, probably a presentation *fraktur*, is here accompanied by a familiar text in cursive form, "Give Jesus your heart in joy and pain, in life or death, this one thing is necessary." (Courtesy of the Rare Book Department, Free Library of Philadelphia, No. FLP 586)

Figure 84: Hereford Township artist. *Vorschrift*, early nineteenth century (20.6 cm. x 30.5 cm., 8" x 12"). Other teachers used the introductory lines of the Gospel of John as the basis for *Vorschriften*. A 1773 example in the Free Library of Philadelphia collection (Fig. 249 in Weiser/Heaney) quotes a single verse (John 1:9), while this text is much more extensive, citing also lines 10–18, beginning with the words, "Christ is the true light that came into this world. . . ." (Courtesy of the Schwenkfelder Library and Heritage Center)

Figure 85: Anonymous. *Vorschrift*, 1827 (19.3 cm. x 32.8 cm., 7.5" x 13"). "He carried his poor lost sheep which went astray. . . ." The image of Jesus as shepherd, prominent in early Christian writing and art, here formulated in the body of a school text: "The noble shepherd, God's Son . . . carried his poor lost sheep which went astray on earth." (Courtesy of the Rare Book Department, Free Library of Philadelphia, No. FLP 335)

Figure 86: David Kriebel. Drawing, 1806 (13.5 cm. x 28.7 cm., 13.5" x 11.25"). Jesus as flower, a theme in devotional poetry and hymnody, expressed here in the text accompanying David Kriebel's floral drawing: "a little flower . . . sprang up in Christ's humanity." (Courtesy of the Schwenkfelder Library and Heritage Center)

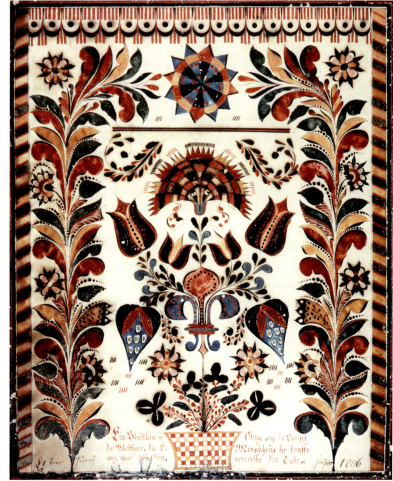

tury, by Ambrose of Milan among others (McCulloch, p. 21). There are several versions of the Latin *Physiologus*, and many of these were likely the sources for medieval bestiaries composed in England and France. In view of such cross-fertilization of images, it is not inconceivable that the *Physiologus* was to have a broader influence on poetry and visual imagery well into the post-Renaissance period, contributing to that great inventory of images which was to take visual form in the *fraktur* of Germany, Pennsylvania, and Ontario

The pelican pecking its breast would appear to be an image derived from *Physiologus*. In the typical *Physiologus* manuscript, the section begins with a biblical quotation, to immediately establish the religious allegorical connection: "I am like a pelican of the wilderness" (Psalm 101:7). Then follows the formula, "*Physiologus* says," describing characteristics of the pelican—that it is loving of its young, and that children begin to grow and actually will strike the parents in the face. The young are then in turn struck and killed. On the third day the parent will pierce its side and spill its blood on the dead offspring, restoring them to life. The text then returns to a biblical reference: "I have nourished and brought up children, and they have rebelled against me" (Isaiah 1:2). The text makes a comparison with humankind's rebellion, striking Christ, thereby incurring death, and then proceeding to the statement that upon the occasion of the Crucifixion, the blood and water of salvation flowed forth from the wound on the side of Christ and gave new life. In such typical explanations, *Physiologus* makes allegorical connections between nature and divine action, as Christian scriptural exegesis of the time was inclined to make connections between Old Testament prophecy and New Testament events.

Possibly the earliest *fraktur* images of the pelican are those found in the illuminated manuscripts of the Ephrata Cloister. A finely detailed drawing of a pelican feeding its young appears in the 1739 *Zionitischer Weyrauchs-Hügel* and again in the 1747 *Das Gesäng der einsamen und verlassenen Turtel-Taube* (fig. 82). The pelican occurs again in several small drawings, probably presentation *frakturs* given by teachers to pupils (fig. 83). Ontario's Anna Weber rendered a simplified version of the motif resembling a cross between a pelican and a Henrich Otto parrot (fig. 119). Drawn in 1876, this may well be one of the last manifestations of this design motif in *fraktur*.

Flower

As the Cross of Christ was frequently compared to a tree in early Christian art, so Jesus is sometimes described as a flower. A noteworthy Pennsylvania *fraktur* representation and text is a Schwenkfelder drawing made in 1806 by David Kriebel. Under a large flower in a basket appears the text: "A little flower is the wisdom that was always with God, sprang up in Christ's humanity, whose strength drives away death" (fig. 86).

Good Shepherd

The Good Shepherd is one of many which early Christianity borrowed from Roman art, casting it in a new Christian interpretation. While the visual image appears to be unknown in Pennsylvania *fraktur*, there are several textual expressions of the motif. An anonymous 1827 *Vorschrift* in the Free Library of Philadelphia reads: "The noble shepherd, God's Son. . . . He carried his poor lost sheep which had gone astray" (fig. 85).

The Suffering Christ

A Pennsylvania *Vorschrift* dated January 22, 1800 (Free Library of Philadelphia Collection, illustrated in Weiser/Heaney, fig. 1107) takes the form of a prayer, emphasizing the suffering of Jesus while at the same time seeking comfort for one's own afflictions:

*Jesus, may your holy wounds,
your agony and bitter death
give me comfort in all times
of physical or spiritual need.*

This is a comparatively gentle document compared to late medieval and Counter-Reformation emphases on the Passion of Christ which, as Don Yoder puts it in his study of the art of Ludwig Denig, "grew into a veritable cult of wounds and blood...." (*Picture-Bible*, p. 57). To be certain, Gothic art had frequently turned toward a preoccupation with the agony of Jesus, paralleling the mystical writings and visions of St. Francis of Assisi and St. Bridget of Sweden. In the sixteenth century, largely under Jesuit influences during the Roman Catholic Counter Reformation, the suffering theme returned in depictions of Jesus as the Man of Sorrows, in images of the *Ecce Homo* biblical passages describing the scourged and suffering Jesus presented to Pilate, and of the bleeding head of Christ looking upwards to Heaven, popularized by El Greco and other artists of the period. How it came to America may have several explanations, not the least of which is the centrality of this imagery in the writings and hymns of Count Nikolaus von Zinzendorff (1700–1760) and in the outlook of his Moravian followers, described by Yoder as "the storm center of blood-and-wounds theology among Protestants" (Yoder, *Picture-Bible*, p. 59). It appears that Zinzendorf was quite fond of having his viewpoint designated as "blood and wounds theology," particularly with regard to his emphasis upon the theme that the blood of Christ is able to cleanse men from their sins by means of a strange mystical power (Stoeffler, "Mysticism," p. 87).

It is known that Zinzendorf also paid a visit to the Ephrata Cloister in 1742, suggesting that his theological point of view would also have been known within the Ephrata Brotherhood as well. Indeed, Conrad Beissel's hymn "Wo geh ich hin" in the 1747 *Turtel-Taube* (cf. New York Pulbic Library MS "KD 1747, No. 410"), a mournfully haunting meditation on the wounds of Christ, testifies to the centrality of this subject in Ephrata hymnody.

The suffering of Christ was a popular theme in Pietism generally, appearing notably in the writings of Johann Arndt, where he writes, "The suffering of Christ is both a payment

Figure 87: Huppert Cassel. Text for Isaac Heebner, 1767 (17.6 cm. x 17.7 cm., 7" x 7").
The Pietistic image of Jesus as personal friend appears in numerous Pennsylvania *fraktur* texts. Huppert Cassel, a Mennonite schoolmaster, has written: "Jesus, come to me . . . come dear friend of the soul, the most beloved which my heart imagines." (Courtesy of the Schwenkfelder Library and Heritage Center)

95

Figure 88: Durs Rudy. Text and drawing of Jesus teaching, early nineteenth century (22.3 cm. x 16.8 cm., 8.75" x 6.50").
Jesus as teacher is the role in which Durs Rudy has chosen to portray him. He shows Jesus preaching to eleven of his disciples, Judas having already left the fold through his betrayal. (Courtesy of the Rare Book Department, Free Library of Philadelphia, No. FLP 309)

for all our sin and a renewing of man through faith" (*Vom Wahren Christentum*, p. 20 [quoted in Stoeffler, p. 98]). Arndt's book was found in households of most Protestant denominations in the Pennsylvania German countryside, and found its way to Ontario with Mennonites migrating to Canada after 1786.

While the visual image is virtually absent from *fraktur* illuminations, it is nonetheless an important subject of its texts. It appears occasionally as a brief reminder contained with documents addressing broader subjects. The Andreas Bauer "clockwork" of 1832 (fig. 128), for example, makes reference to the "five wounds of Christ" in its twelve reflections upon the hours of the day.

Yoder's claim that graphic visual representation of the suffering of Christ was abandoned in Protestant art is contradicted by the presence of crucifixes in many Lutheran churches in Germany, a feature made visible in details of a church interior shown in collage-like manner in a *fraktur* by Arnold Hoevelmann (Wichman Collection). The suffering Christ dominates the verses appearing in various Pennsylvania German hymnbooks. The hymn "Jesu meines Leben's Leben" in *Lutheran Erbauliche Liedersammlung* as well as the Mennonite *Zionsharfe* and *Unpartheyisches Gesangbuch* reminds us of the fact of Jesus' suffering in elaborate detail: Important here, as in the *Vorschrift* of 1800, is the consoling role of the words, in which the believer is reminded of the redemptive purpose of the suffering willingly endured by Christ:

> *Thou, oh thou, hast on thee taken*
> *Blasphemy, mockery and scorn,*
> *Spittle, smiting, scourging chain bound*
> *Thou, the Righteous, God's own Son. . . .*
>
> *Thou allowed those wounds to smite Thee,*
> *Execution, wretchedness.*
> *Thus to heal that which has plagued me,*
> *And to set my heart at rest. . . .*
>
> *Man with scoffings harshly mocked Thee,*
> *Heaped upon you shameful scorn,*
> *And with piercing thorns they crowned Thee,*
> *What the reason this was borne?*
> *To delight me, Thou hast chosen*
> *Me, thine own, with honor to crown.*
>
> *From my heart I truly thank Thee,*
> *For what Thou suffered with each breath,*
> *For Thy wounds, painful agony,*
> *For Thy harsh and bitter death.*
> *For Thy tremblings, dreadful fearings,*
> *For Thy thousand awful sufferings*
> *For Thy woe and deepest pain*
> *E'ver thankful I'll remain.*
> (Transl., Stoltzfuss, pp. 42–43)

Figure 89: Anonymous. Presentation *fraktur*, 1790 (14.8 cm. x 8.4 cm., 5.75" x 3").
A devotional motto inscribed in the hymnal of Maria Clemer addresses Jesus as teacher: "Christ's teaching shows me the way. . . . Through the Spirit, O Lord, teach me, so that I know you aright and do your will at all times, so that when you come, I am ready." (Courtesy of the Rare Book Department, Free Library of Philadelphia, No. FLP B-1002)

Figure 90: Attributed to Joel Cassel. *Vorschrift*, 1841 (20 cm. x 32 cm., 7.75" x 12.25").
Very much in the tradition of late-medieval emphasis upon the suffering of Christ is Joel Cassel's *Vorschrift*: "Jesus, may thy holy wounds, thy torture and bitter death, Console me every hour in times of bodily and spiritual need." (Courtesy of the Spruance Library of the Bucks County Historical Society)

These themes of suffering and salvation are expressed even toward mid-century in an 1841 *Vorschrift* when once again a *fraktur*-scrivener has used as his source the Pietist hymn "*Jesu deine heilige Wunden*": The hymnist had not shown the least hesitation to use the strong word *Quall* (translated above as "agony," but equally readable as "torture"), appearing here in a text made for or by Joel Cassell (fig. 90):

Jesus, may thy holy wounds, thy torture and bitter death,
Console me every hour in times of bodily and spiritual need.

The significance of these seemingly morose descriptions lies in both the redemptive role of suffering and of its everyday catalytic effect of reminding the believer to remain steadfast in faith:

When the world seeks to lead me astray
onto the broad path of sin,
Wilt Thou then govern me that I may behold
the heavy burden of Thy agony which you have endured,
So that I can remain devout and drive away every evil desire.

Many are the faces of Jesus appearing in these texts, rooted variously in the orthodoxy of early patristic theology or in the personalism of eighteenth-century Pietism. The variety of images suggests something of the ambiguity of Pennsylvania German religious generally, with its theological tensions between denominational particularism and the generalized Jesus theology of Pietistic spirituality.

Figure 91: Anonymous. Bookplate, 1849 (17 cm. x 21.8 cm., 10" x 8.5"). From the Patristic Era forward, references to Jesus as the Second Adam abounded in writings, art, and as popular figure of speech. Here, on a bookplate for Johannes and Anna Denlinger, the text reads, "What Adam spoiled, Jesus won back." (Courtesy of the Rare Book Department, Free Library of Philadelphia, No. FLP 699)

Figure 92: John Zinck. Birth record for David Royer, circa 1811.
John Zinck's English-language *fraktur* record has abandoned all pretenses at being religiously motivated, restricting its interest here to that of recording the birth of David Royer. The mortality theme is once again prominent in the reminder that "we're trav'lling to the grave." (Collection of Richard S. and Rosemarie B. Machmer)

CHAPTER V

LIFE'S JOURNEYS: STAGES, PATHS, MAZES, AND LABYRINTHS

There are two ways in the present day
The one narrow, the other wide,
Who now will go the narrow way,
Will be by everyone despised.

This plainly God's Word teaches us,
Enter in by the narrow way
Straight is the gate, who will enter
Must first great suffering endure.
—Hymn, "Es sind zween Weg in dieser Zeit,"
Ausbund, no. 125)

Enter ye in at the strait gate; for wide is the gate and broad is the way that leadeth to destruction; and many there be which go in there. Because strait is the gate, and narrow is the way, which leadeth unto life, and few there be that find it.
—Matthew: 7:13–14

The marking of life's thresholds is an ancient practice in virtually all religions of the world, grounded in the understanding that the religious dimension of experience entails degrees of progression, advancement, enrichment, or deepening of insight. In the Christian theological tradition the journey is understood against the backdrop of human sin and separation from God. Earthly life is regarded as a sojourn through a temporary world toward the promise of reconciliation through the grace of God, and in the context of the religious community, the journey is witnessed by the rituals and recording of the major events of birth, baptism, and other stages along life's way. Other events may include marriage, and—in the Church traditions—the sacramental event of Confirmation. *Fraktur* documents, both printed and hand-lettered, witness also the fact of death and texts frequently emphasize the promise of life beyond the grave and reconciliation of the pilgrim with God in Paradise. *Fraktur* forms which serve the purpose of the marking of life's events include birth records, baptismal certificates, family records, Confirmation texts, marriage records, texts on death, and the promise of afterlife.

Figure 93: Isaac Z. Hunsicker. Family record, circa 1850.
Like their New England counterparts, Pennsylvania Germans were interested in maintaining geneaological records. Isaac Hunsicker has here recorded the marriage of David and Magdalena (Martin) Horst and the births of their children in Waterloo County, Ontario. (Courtesy of the Canadian Harvest Collection, Joseph Schneider Haus Museum)

Figure 94: Attributed to Mahantongo Valley artist.
Taufschein, circa 1833.
Although the collection of images on this form may be random, there is nonetheless a significant connection between the record of birth and baptism and the image of Noah's ark as a well-known epic story of rebirth. (Private Collection)

Figure 95: Anonymous. Birth-and-baptismal certificate for Daniel Moser, circa 1810 (22 cm. x 35 cm., 8.375" x 13.75").
A *Taufschein* which, though it omits the date of baptism, has been updated to indicate that the seventeen-year-old Daniel Moser was baptized on Good Friday in 1813, and "on Easter Sunday he received Holy Communion from Pastor Mennig." (Courtesy of the Ungerbassler Collections, Phillips Museum of Art, Franklin and Marshall College)

Figure 96: Daniel Schumacher. Confirmation certificate for Maria Magdalena Spengler, circa 1780. Confirmation is the central subject (rather than added information of a *Taufschein*) in this certificate by Daniel Schumacher. The confirmation of Maria Spengler in 1780 has set her securely on her "heavenly journey" with full entry into the adult community of faith. (Private Collection)

Figure 97: Attributed to Daniel Diefenbach. Marriage record, circa 1826.
Marriage was not a sacrament in Protestant churches, but the event was sometimes recorded on *fraktur* documents, much as were births and genealogies. (Private Collection)

Figure 98: George Anders. Text, "Devotions on Dying," 1750–52 (15.3 cm. x 19.5 cm., 6" x 7.25").
Among early Schwenkfelders who made hand-lettered copies of theological works brought along from Europe, George Anders was important, notably for his texts on devotions on dying and sermons for burials. This *Sterbens Andacht* quotes Psalm 90, "Lord, teach us to number our days that we may receive a heart of wisdom." (Courtesy of the Schwenkfelder Library and Heritage Center)

Figure 99: Peter Montelius. Printed *Memento Mori*, circa 1837.
The term *Denkmal* is typically associated with the idea of memorializing, translated as *monument* or even *gravemarker*. This printed text, honoring the death of Friederich Kobel in Northumberland County, is fittingly placed within a tombstone-like framework. (Courtesy of Special Collections, Franklin and Marshall College)

Figure 100: Anonymous. Death record, 1771.
In form this hand-drawn record of death made at Germantown resembles baroque memorial tablets. Words at the top link the fact of death to Original Sin. A central panel is reserved for the name of the deceased, flanked by grim images of skulls and coffin. More uplifting is the text which offers hope to the faithful: "Death is bitter as gall to those separated from God; But death is sweet to those who die in Jesus." (Courtesy of Special Collections, Beeghly Library, Juniata College, Huntingdon, Pennsylvania; photography by Dr. Donald Durnbaugh)

Figure 102: Susanna Heebner. Labyrinth, circa 1807–1810 (16.9 cm. x 20.8 cm., 6.75" x 8.50"). Copied from a page in Johannes Tauler's *Helleleüchtender Herzens'-Spiegel* (1680), this hand-drawn labyrinth by Susanna Heebner dwells upon the theme of the pathway and the need to follow Jesus. The text is concluded by a quotation from Matthew 19:21, "Go Sell, give and come follow me. Jesus." (Courtesy of the Schwenkfelder Library and Heritage Center)

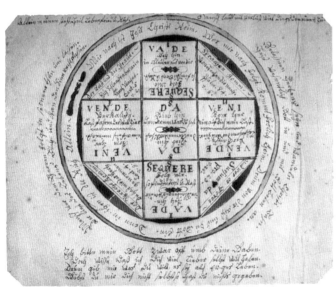

Figure 101: Anonymous. Religious text (Ephrata Cloister), circa 1750 (18 cm. x 22 cm., 7" x 8.5") While the Confirmation certificate (Fig. 96) referred to the *Himmelsfahrt* or heavenly journey, this Ephrata Cloister text makes explicit the hope of resurrection after death: "At the end of the rough pilgrim's path my goal will be reached." (Courtesy of the Rare Book Department, Free Library of Philadelphia, No. FLP 710)

105

A different category of *fraktur* texts serves not so much the recording function of life's stages as the exhorting function of the believer to consider the divergent pathways presenting themselves along the journey. It is to these texts, taking variously the forms of puzzles, double-path choices, mazes, and labyrinths, that attention will be turned in the consideration of the road along which the spiritual journey might be traveled.

The theme of the "two ways" can be traced to the earliest generations of Christian believers, and in fact to the accounts of the Passion, in which Jesus assured the repentant thief of that he would enter into Heaven. Scriptural references to "path" metaphor are surprisingly few in number and of brief duration. Matthew's two-verse description of the straight gate and the wide narrow path has its even briefer parallel in a short quotation in Luke 13:14, and both may hearken back to a Deuteronomic text, where Yahweh speaks to Israel on the subject of the need for repentance. The language of Deuteronomy is social, whereas that of Matthew and Luke is personal. Israel must make a choice between obedience and idolatry. The rewards and punishments are of enormous consequence: "I set before you this day life and goodness or death and evil" (Deuteronomy 30:15). The people of Israel are cautioned in these lines of Deuteronomy that what is required is repentance, a righting of wrong ways, and obedience to God. In Mark and Luke, Jesus presents a similar choice to individual listeners, but goes beyond Deuteronomy's straightforward articulation of choices to point out that in fact humanity may find one option more difficult than other, the path of righteousness entailing entry through a straight gate and along a narrow path.

In the hymnody and sometimes the *fraktur* texts of the Pennsylvania Germans, the theme of two ways may have struck a particularly strong resonance with a number of prevailing themes. Some of these have earlier theological roots, but were no doubt reinforced by the broad influence of Pietism. Noteworthy in this regard are themes of ethical conduct, turning spiritually inwards, undergoing an experience of repentance, and a sense that true religion means a turning away from the imperfections of the world.

The theme of repentance lurks behind many *fraktur* texts. Sometimes it does not lurk so much as leap out. To the extent that life is understood as a preparation for eternity, perhaps no form of preparedness can be as important as that of the truly repentant heart, contrite at every moment. Mention has already been made of the line on a 1798 "Spiritual Clockworks" *fraktur* attributed to Johannes Moyer: *Mensch von Herzens Grund/Ihre Buss zu aller Stund*—"O

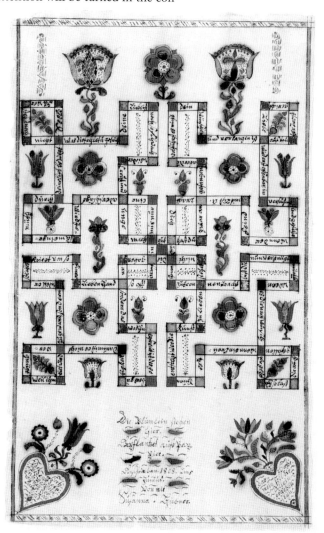

Figure 103: Susanna Heebner. Labyrinth, 1808 (34 cm. x 20.6 cm., 13.5" x 8").
Though the believer may get off to a good start in the journey of life, many are the challenges to staying on the path. "You have indeed started well, but you don't act on it (love) .... Love first becomes evident in temptation and danger when the enemy tries to separate you and me...." (Courtesy of the Schwenkfelder Library and Heritage Center)

man, from the bottom of your heart, repent every hour" (fig. 127). F. Ernest Stoeffler and Don Yoder have argued that there is a trinity of Pietistic themes emanating from the writings of principal writers such as Johann Arndt (1555–1621), and which were filtered through hymns and popular spirituality in Pennsylvania, including *Busse* ("repentance"), *Abkehr* ("turning away from the world") and *Einkehr* ("turning inward"). It is interesting that in those rare pictorial treatments of the Crucifixion in *fraktur*, artist Arnold Puwelle has chosen to weigh the scene with Jesus's words of assurance of heavenly reward to the thief who was repentant (fig. 72).

The process of repentance, turning away and turning in can be seen as the spiritual acts which are in accordance with the choice of the narrow path and the straight gate. The two-path theme was used by Johan Tauler (1300–1361) in his description of the alternative routes which present themselves to the pilgrim (A page from the 1680 printing of Tauler's *Helleleüchtender Hertzens-Spiegel* is shown in Moyer, p. 85, and is included in the author's discussion of printed sources for *fraktur* by Susanna Heebner). Being the mystic he was, Tauler connects the imagery of the Gospels with lines in the Apocalypse: "Be faithful unto death, and I will give you the crown of life" (Revelation 2:10). Tauler also cites the well-known passages in the Gospel of Matthew (7:13) and adds his commentary, "Would you be cool or hot (that is, inclined toward the temperatures of heaven or hell)?" The greatest religious sin is that of indifference, with further citation from Matthew 3:15–16: "Because you are lukewarm, I will spew you out of my mouth." Tauler's development of this theme consists of a systematic integration of several scriptural sources, including passages from the first Psalm: "For the Lord knows that way of the righteous, but the way of the wicked will perish (Psalm 1:6).

Tauler's 1680 text and engraving of the two roads, one leading to eternal life, the other to damnation, would appear to have inspired numerous Pennsylvania German printers and artists. Moyer observes that the subject of the path to heaven or hell had gained a degree of popularity in Pennsylvania through the medium of broadsides published in the early nine-

Figure 104: Anonymous. Labyrinth, 1772 (19 cm. x 19.2 cm., 7.5" x 7.5").
Labyrinths were made for both secular and religious love, the former as valentines, the latter as spiritual texts. The words here are similar to those in figure 103, including the spiritual observation, "The one who knows the art of love does not look at the gifts but is delighted with the giver." (Courtesy of the Schwenkfelder Library and Heritage Center)

teenth century (Moyer, p. 84). It also influenced Schwenkfelder artist Susanna Heebner, who executed a hand-drawn adaptation circa 1807–1810 (fig. 106). In both examples—the printed original and the hand-drawn interpretation—the narrow path begins in a cultivated field and leads to a crown of glory, while the wide path is placed in an overgrown wilderness and leads to a crown of flames. Both texts conclude with that unequivocal decision-forcing charge from Yahweh to Israel: ". . . therefore choose life, that you and your descendants may live" (Fifth Book of Moses 30:19) (Deuteronomy 30:19).

While the two-path imagery of book engraving, printed broadside, and hand-lettered *fraktur* indicate something of the prevalence of this theme in Pennsylvania German culture, there was another image for the spiritual journey which may have gained wider popularity in *fraktur* drawings. This alternative form was rendered in the form of a maze or labyrinth, frequently given a descriptive title, *Irrgarten*. In the labyrinthine format, the idea of choosing one of two paths was replaced with an emphasis upon the challenges comprising the journey along the "proper" path, the road described as "narrow" and "difficult." The word *labyrinth* may be problematic in that the term has a more specific connotation than the more general word *maze*. Historically, the *labyrinth* is associated with a particular form originating in Crete and with specific descriptions as to how it is laid out and the details of a path leading in and path leading out (for a more detailed study of the labyrinth in Western cultural history, cf. Purce, *The Mystic Spiral*). A maze, by contrast, may take almost any form in which one must travel from one point to another by a route marked by twists, turns, obstacles, and challenges.

An anonymous text, dated 1772 (fig. 104), proposes that the believer is unaware of what is needed to complete the journey, having an idea of the elements of love, but not fully understanding the importance of knowing the one who gives such love. The metaphor of searching is developed in the words: "You have indeed started well, but you do not carry through." Perhaps like the traveler who wanders too quickly onto the wide and "easy" path, the soul is subjected to deception: "Love first becomes evident in temptation and danger when the enemy tries to separate you and me with ruse and might" (is the "Me" Jesus himself?). This language of starting, getting off on a wrong foot, succumbing to distractions, but being offered the possibility of safe arrival by turning attention to the Giver is given a formal parallel in the design of the text itself. The words are laid out in pathways which meander and reverse themselves many times before eventually reaching the end. Form and content convey to the reader the sense that the journey is indeed labyrinthine, a puzzle, and a challenge to turn from human to divine wisdom.

A somewhat similar example from 1813 (fig. 105) uses the device of a "woven" path which continually changes direction. Its text emphasizes the challenge of staying on the true path, given many temptations along the way. "Man, have you desire to travel? Hear how you must travel in the world and in sins. . . ." We are given a vivid description of

Figure 105: Anonymous. *Irrgarten*, circa 1813 (32 cm. x 30 cm., 12.5" x 12").

The religious significance of the labyrinthine journey through the *Irrgarten* (garden of errors) is here made explicit in terms of a medieval concept, the *via crucis*. "The way of the cross is solitary, deep, narrow and stark. . . ." (Courtesy of the Rare Book Department, Free Library of Philadelphia, No. FLP 79)

temptations, and instructed: "Pay no heed to whoever is at the side, Only look in front of you quietly and gently." The image is reminiscent in late medieval art of Albrecht Dürer's *Knight, Death and the Devil*, in which he is challenged to look straight ahead and not the side where he might be led astray from his religious goal.

In medieval Catholicism, the popularity of pilgrimages such as those to Canterbury or Santiago da Compostella reflect an ancient notion of wishing to walk in the footsteps of Jesus. When matters of distance and military danger discouraged journeys to the Holy Land itself, local pilgrimages provided an alternative means of following the Way of the Cross, or *Via Crucis*. The miniaturization of such pilgrimages took the form of the Devotions of the Stations of the Cross, in which believers could walk through the story of the Passion by circumambulating the interior of the church, stopping at each Station to reflect upon the meaning of the particular events in Jesus' own journey to Golgotha. The 1813 *Irrgarten* text cited here goes so far as to make a connection to medieval practice, using the language of *Via Crucis*: "And the way of the cross is solitary, deep, narrow and stark. . . ." It quotes as its source a German prayerbook, the *Geistliches Blumen Gärtlein* ("The Spiritual Blooming Garden") reprinted in the New World by Christoph Saur in 1747. In order to get through the maze successfully, one thing is necessary: "Let yourself be faithful to the leader. . . ." and "Let Jesus be your guide."

The labyrinth had pre-Christian roots in the worlds of Crete, Greece, and Rome, but was integrated within the theological understanding of the "difficult path." On occasion, the Cretan labyrinth form found its way into the heart of the cathedral, as in the enormous stone labyrinth set into the floor of Chartres Cathedral. When the worshipper enters Chartres Cathedral and proceeds in an easterly direction toward the high altar, almost universally understood as a symbolic process from earth to Heaven, it was necessary to cross the labyrinth enroute. In so doing, the believer might well be reminded of the difficult and indirect nature of the true path to Salvation.

Perhaps the most explicit description of the labyrinthan religious journey is to be found in a printed *Irrgarten* published by Henrich Otto, circa 1784 (fig. 107). This printed *Geistlicher Irrgarten* refers to the very process by which it ought to be read: "The tortuous course which the reading takes characterizes the many and varied cares and afflictions of this life. . . ." Like the hand-drawn *Irrgarten* of 1813, the Otto printed form emphasizes the role of divine guidance, which when heard by the pilgrim lead to the affirmative proclamation, "Now I have hope of coming to the right path and way, that I may get out of the garden maze."

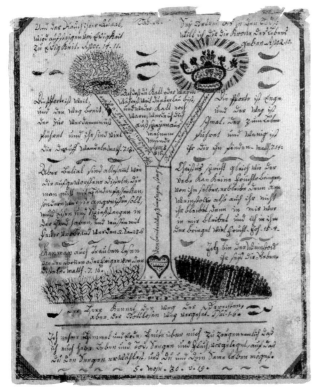

Figure 106: Susanna Heebner. Text, ***Path of Heaven or Hell****, circa 1807–1810 (20.2 cm. x 17 cm., 8" x 6.75"). The artist Susanna Heebner has once again drawn from the Tauler volume used for the labyrinth in Fig. 102. Here she has copied his engraved image of the path to heaven or hell, one leading to desolation, the other to the crown of glory. There are many scriptural references here, and repeated warnings that the wide gate and easy path lead to destruction, while the narrow gate and difficult path lead to salvation. (Courtesy of the Schwenkfelder Library and Heritage Center)**

A last category of *fraktur* compositions whose form parallels the notion of the difficult journey is that loosely described as "puzzles," of which many varieties abound. An interesting example is the Durs Rudy metamorphic puzzle of 1832 (cf. fig. 40). It takes the form of a puzzle book with turn-up pages, by which the reader attempts to follow the narrative of human history contained therein. The theme is the familiar Christian account of Creation, Fall, human history, and return to the Kingdom of God. Pages can be turned up in various combinations, leading from one event to another. The images and texts are very similar to those found in early New England primers, translated into German when the image became popular in Pennsylvania. Durs Rudy's metamorphic version emphasizes the urgency of choice of the ways of repentance and faithfulness against the distractions and temptations of earthly life. The composition is in effect a riddle, with instructions as to how to lift particular pages and learn of truths hidden beneath. Like primers, the text is strongly didactic, and the puzzle form becomes a metaphor for the challenges along the way in life's journey.

A final example of the puzzle is another Susanna Heebner composition, copied from yet another page in Johan Tauler (fig. 102). The text makes abundant reference to wandering and traveling, and especially to the importance of "following the heart." The text reads, "To have a calm heart and wander on Christ's path means mainly to worship in God and with God." Following the text requires the reader to turn the composition sideways and upside down. Close inspection of Latin words beginning and ending with the exhortation to "follow me" reveals that the first letter of these phrases taken together makes up the name *Jesus*. The idea of hidden words made up of first letters of phrases is not unique to this example, of course. A similar device is to be found in the religious text constructed as a "Golden ABC," wherein the first initials of words in successive passages make up the letters of the alphabet from A to Z. The final lines of the Susanna Heebner composition are taken from Matthew 19:21, indicating the radical choice that ultimately must be made: "go and sell that thou hast, and give to the poor . . . and come and follow me."

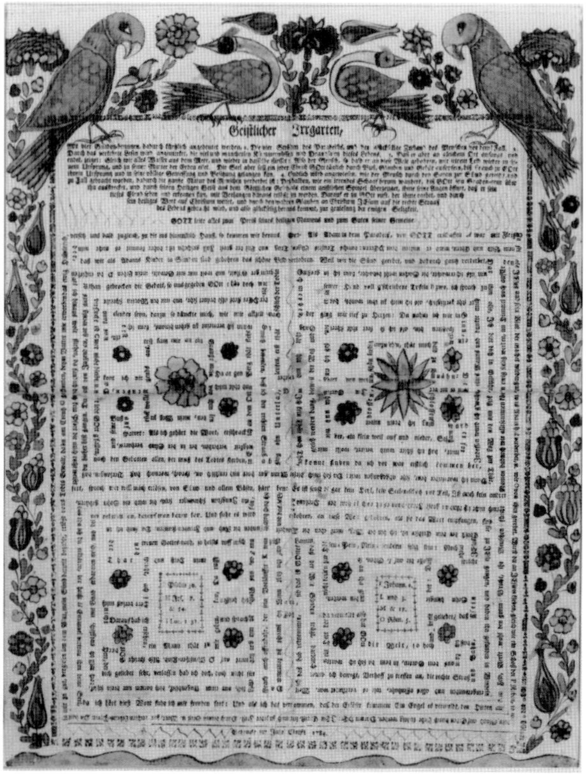

Words deliberately scrambled as a challenge for the reader serve a wide range of purposes, from simple entertainment for children to philosophical and theological challenges for adult readers. The Jewish tradition of gematria, a mystical technique of biblical exegesis, searches for deeper meanings in scripture by substitution of numbers for letters in the Hebrew text. In broader contexts, a particularly interesting word game takes the form of the *palindrome* (Latin—"to walk back again"). Here, words are gathered together in such a way that a text can be read from front to back or back to front. A classic and popular example is "Madam I'm Adam" or "Able was I ere I saw Elba."

Figure 107: Henrich Otto. Spiritual garden maze (broadside), circa 1784 (41 cm. x 32 cm., 16" x 12.25"). The text gives explanation to the format: "The tortuous course the reading takes characterizes the many and varied cares and afflictions of this life. . . ." It goes on to describe the wanderer's thoughts: "I saw a garden in the distance. . . . I felt I could very nearly get lost in it. . . . Eventually, divine words of assurance are head by the pilgrim, who then says, "Now I have hopes of coming to the right path and way, that I may get out of the garden maze." (Courtesy of the Winterthur Museum)

While many of the most famous English-language palindromes are little more than structural play, some palindromes include content within their schemata of forward/reversal as well, as in the expression: *Dog as a devil deified; deified lived as a god*. Here, not only is there formal juxtaposition of opposite movements; there is also a polarization of imagery, with *dog* and *God* placed at opposite ends, and with counterposturing of *devil* and *deified*.

Like visual forms of symmetry (notably *fraktur* compositions!) palindromic narrative forms perform the paradoxical function of suggesting the one embracing the two, and the centre uniting opposite movements.

During that period in which late Antiquity overlapped early Christianity there developed a most remarkable example of a palindrome expressing an explicit religious theme. In locations as diverse as Pompeii and Cirencester there appears a Latin palindrome in the following form:

```
S A T O R
T E N E T
O P E R A
R O T A S
```

Reading from top to bottom, bottom to top, left to right, right to left, the pattern is that of a palindrome which, translated, states, "Arepo the sower holds the wheels to the work" (for a fuller discussion of this palindrome, see Caviness). This seemingly mundane observation can be seen, however, to convey a much deeper meaning, alluding to the themes of Faith, the Lord's Prayer, Crucifixion, the Eternity of God and the hope of Salvation. The first of these themes is suggested by the central cross-within-the-square, comprised of the intersecting words *tenet* and *tenet* ("to hold, as in a held belief"). While other words are palindromes only when taken together as pairs (*sator* and *rotas*, for example, or *opera* and *arepo*), the word *tenet* is a self-contained palindrome.

```
        T
        E
T E N E T
        E
        T
```

The first two words of the Lord's Prayer, *pater noster* ("Our Father") are found when all the letters (except four) in the square are rearranged to form a larger cross:

```
            P
            A
            T
            E
            R
P A T E R N O S T E R
            O
            S
            T
            E
            R
```

The four omitted letters are of considerable significance. They are the letters A, O, A, O, the first and last letters of the Greek alphabet, *alpha* and *omega*. In Christian symbolism, the pairing of these letters alludes to the Eternity of God, hearkening to the Biblical reference, "I am the alpha and the omega, the beginning and the end" (Revelation 21:6). The placement of the *alpha* and *omega* on the ends of the cross as a symbol of eternity beyond the crucifixion is a recurring feature of Christian art, found variously on sarcophagi and mosaics at Ravenna or on medieval church tympana. The palindrome now appears as follows:

```
                                    P
                                    A
                                    T
                            A       E       O
                                    R
    S A T O R                       
    A R E P O               P A T E R N O S T E R
    T E N E T                       O
    O P E R A                       S
    R O T A S               A       T       O
                                    E
                                    R
```

An interesting variation on this ancient cryptogram found its way into the *fraktur* workmanship of Johannes Spangenberg when he used it as the format for a hand-drawn composition done in the late eighteenth century (fig. 108). Most likely his source was an engraved image found perhaps in a book context or even as a printed broadside. What is immediately noticeable is that the text has undergone modification at several places. The letter *p* in *arepo* and *opera* has been replaced with a *t*, and *tenet* has been changed to *heset*, all nonsensical words. Only a hint of the palindromic puzzle remains with the center word no longer readable in both directions. Still, the reader is drawn to the challenge of deciphering those words juxtaposed in ascending and descending pattern, and one still senses that the text is intended as at least a mental teaser, if not also some deeper philosophic mystery.

Figure 108: Johannes Spangenberg. Palindromic text, late eighteenth century.
An ancient text from antiquity, adapted in early Christian contexts, invited the observer to decode the puzzle by reading from both ends (and also from top and bottom) toward the center. The original text read *sator arepo tenet opera rotas* **("Arepo the sower holds the wheel to his work. . . ."), an allusion to the importance of holding to articles ("tenets") of faith. Somewhere in the Pennsylvania setting the text was further modified, as in this hand-lettered version by Spangenberg. (Private Collection)**

In various manifestations, each of these *fraktur* compositions provides a formal equivalence to its message. The theme of choice between the road to heaven and the road to hell is expressed in text and echoed in the stylistic counterparts of map-like depictions of two paths, or labyrinthan arrangement of words, or as enigmas to be solved by rotation or turning-up of pages. In this way, they offer insights into the idea that it is the difficult, not the easy road, which leads to spiritual fulfillment.

Found in *Ausbund* and *Liedersammlung*:

(Holy Bible: International Children's Version)
Luke 13:24
Jesus said, "Try hard to enter through the narrow door that opens the way to heaven! Many people will try there, but they will not be able."

Matthew 7:13
Enter through the narrow gate. The road that leads to hell is a very easy road. And the gate to hell is very wide. Many people enter through that gate.

Matthew 7:14
But the gate that opens the way to true life is very small. And the road to true life is very hard. Only a few people find that road.

(Holy Bible: King James Version)
Luke 13:24
Strive to enter in at the strait gate: for many, I say unto you, will seek to enter in, and shall not be able.

Matthew 7:13
Enter ye in at the strait gate: for wide is the gate, and broad is the way, that leadeth to destruction, and many there be which go in thereat. . . .

Matthew 7:14
Because strait is the gate, and narrow is the way, which leadeth unto life, and few there be that find it.

Peake's Commentary
Peake's commentary connects this passage and Luke 13:24 to the text of Deuteronomy 30:15, in which God declares to Israel that it has two choices, the way of life and good or the way of death and evil.

Deuteronomy 30:15
See I have set before thee this day life and good, and death and evil. . . .

Here the reference is to the idea of the Repentance of Israel (in exile). The choice is between obedience to God or false gods—true God or idolatry. There is a righteous way (to God) and an idolatrous way (to false gods).

Figure 109: Susanna Heebner. Text, 1807 (19.7 cm. x 33.5 cm., 7.25" x 13.25").
Even in springtime one has to think of the autumn of life: "For the beautiful May of the fresh years of youth is over quickly. . . . A flower soon fades." The theme of mortality yields in this text to a more hopeful prospect when praying to Jesus: "Implant yourself in me, and I will stay standing forever." (Courtesy of the Schwenkfelder Library and Heritage Center)

CHAPTER VI

MEMENTO MORI/TEMPUS FUGIT:
MORTALITY AND TIME
IN FRAKTUR TEXTS

King, prince, nobleman, peasant,

Old, young, great, small, rich, poor,

All must die. Amen.

In this terse proclamation, artist Anna Weber (1814–1888) has recorded in her own hand the long-familiar text which emphasizes in relentlessly grim terms the theme of death as the great leveler. She has abbreviated somewhat the list of victims, omitting traditional references to pope, freeman, and city-dweller, and has substituted a ring of hearts for the customary circle of skulls (*Schädelkreis*) She has also personalized the formulaic expression by making reference to herself as "an old weak woman of 65" (she was herself sixty-five on the date that she made this drawing). The recipient of this gloomy text was someone barely entering into young womanhood, the sixteen-year-old Amanda Eby whose family lived a few farms away from the artist.

As Frederick Weiser has said elsewhere, in his discussion of another text, "like much fraktur, its content is preoccupied with death. . . ." (Weiser, "Fraktur," p. 237). This seemingly medieval *Memento Mori* theme, with strong antecedents in theological responses to the Plague of the fourteenth century and expressed in mural paintings and woodcuts by Hans Holbein the Younger (1497/8–1543) and others, seems to have undergone a revival of sorts in Pietistic hymnody and devotional poetry in the seventeenth century. It is most likely from this "second" source that the death theme was to make its appearance in Pennsylvania *fraktur* of the eighteenth and nineteenth centuries. When Holbein used the woodcut to make forty representations of Death paying his call, he provided the means by which printed copies could be distributed far and wide. Holbein has already transformed the "Dance of Death" into the depiction of Death as "Harvester" or "Grim Reaper." In this version, Death is shown as a skeleton appearing at inconvenient times to lay claim to persons from all stations of life, reminding us, as expressed in the words printed much later at Ephrata, *Mensch du muss sterben*.

The theme of the Dance of Death as a subject for printed text was a rare phenomenon in Pennsylvania, but did makes its appearance as a broadside, very possibly printed at Ephrata. This late-eighteenth-century broadside is the subject of a discussion by Edgar Breitenbach in "*Des Kaysers Abschied* and the First Dance of Death in America," (p. 4–9) who connects the 1745 Pennsylvania form to an earlier version printed in 1702 in Basel. The Pennsylvania example, titled *Des Kaysers Abschied* ("the Emperor's Farewell"*)*, takes the form of a dialogue between Death and the Emperor, wherein the latter pleads with

Death to allow him to live on. The dialogue with Death is the subject of many medieval morality plays, and has had its most famous cinematic expression in Ingmar Bergman's film *The Seventh Seal*. The Emperor must learn the inevitable fact of his mortality, which in medieval narratives was linked to the Fall and its consequences for future humankind. In *Des Kaysers Abschied*, the Emperor comes to accept his fate courageously and is depicted in his consoling role in comforting the Empress who is present at his deathbed.

Albeit in muted form, the Dance of Death did find its way briefly into Pennsylvania German visual arts. It was one of many religious images rendered on cast-iron stoveplates from the middle to the later eighteenth century. An example described by Henry Mercer in 1899 as an adaptation of a sixteenth-century prototype, once again hearkens back to a source in Basel. The stoveplate tableau features a skeleton holding a leg bone as a club, seizing his richly dressed victim. Death takes away the wealthy man as assuredly as he claims the poor man. A detailed description of probable sources of this pictorial Pennsylvania stoveplate in early engraved images is provided by Henry C. Mercer in his *The Bible in Iron: Pictured Stoves and Stoveplates of the Pennsylvania Germans* (fig. 110).

Figure 110: Elizabeth Martin. Embroidered towel (detail), 1849. The familiar acrostic reminder of death, OEHBDDE (*O Edel Herz Bedenk Dein End*—O Nobel Heart Consider Thy End) is worked in cross-stitch on many Pennsylvania German embroidered towels, such as this example made in Waterloo County, Ontario. (Courtesy of the Canadian Harvest Collection, Joseph Schneider Haus Museum)

Unlike the Dance of Death, which was generally depicted as a series of visits by Death to representative members of society, the *Memento Mori* was typically a single image of Death represented by a skeleton or skull. Even this theme had little place in *fraktur* decoration, although it was a common one in the decoration of tombstones in both English and German cemeteries in New England and the Middle Atlantic States. The strongest visual suggestion of mortality amounts to little more than the circle of skulls (or what may be its modification in fig. 114). A skull and bones focuses attention on the theme of mortality in the death record done at Germantown in 1771 (fig. 100). Resembling a stone memorial tablet of a type found frequently in churches, this paper composition is relentlessly sombre with hand-drawn coffin and skulls surrounding a blank section reserved for the name of the deceased.

In another example (illustrated in Weiser and Heaney as plate 151) the *Memento Mori* idea is suggested by the simple device of the *Schädelkreis* in which the artist has replaced the morbid depiction of skulls with the more appealing arrangement of a circle of faces (fig. 113). Like the Anna Weber drawing, the composition by this artist is most likely derived from an engraved image such as that appearing in several late-eighteenth-century Ephrata publications.

The visual imagery of the death theme in Pennsylvania-German folk art is considerably blunted, especially in *fraktur*; nonetheless, textual references to death and the *Memento Mori* theme can be quite unrestrained in their solemn directness. Several texts on the theme, examined by Don Yoder in "The Fraktur Texts and Pennsylvania-German Spirituality" (Amsler, *Bucks County Fraktur*, pp. 43–62), contain familiar folk motifs, but none specifically associated with death. And yet the texts are uncomfortably realistic and forthright on the subject.

A 1782 *Vorschrift* for the young Abraham Oberholtzer (fig. 116) is graphic in its descriptions: "Not a single small hour passes by in which I can forget that Death will put me in final misery. . . . Death has the power, he wreaks havoc on young and old, he tears us out of our earthly condition and place. . . ." Don Yoder has likened this *fraktur* description to medieval personification of Death as the Grim Reaper and Harvester (Yoder, in Amsler, p. 49). That short introductory reference to *Stündlein* ("small hour") is significant, given the emphasis on the theme of the urgency of time which arises again and again in *fraktur* texts and which is the subject of Spiritual Clockworks in Weiser's *Fraktur*.

A hand-lettered hymn done in 1816 for Jacob Oberholtzer (fig. 117) expresses the situation in terrifyingly psychological terms: "Oh Death! Oh Death! When you call me, I break out into a cold sweat" (Yoder, in Amsler, p. 50). Earlier in this same piece, the text refers to the victim's lament in terms strikingly similar to those of the *Basel Totentanz*, or the words of *Des Kaysers Abschied*, in which the distressed believer feels sorry for his wife and child who weep at the prospect of his death.

The most common textual "wake-up call" in Pennsylvania *fraktur* was the short *Bedenk Dein End* phrase found on bookmarkers and scattered around the margins of longer texts. The text has early musical associations, notably in the late-seventeenth-century hymn "Bedenke, Mensch, das Ende," written by Salomo Liscov (1640–1689), a poet and clergyman near Grimm, Germany. Liscov set the words to the melody used earlier by Bach for his "O Sacred Head Now Wounded," included in the *St. Matthew Passion* of 1729 (cf. Fretz, p. 36). In Pennsylvania, the words were also used by women (and occasionally, men) in the embroidery of linen towels. In this latter instance, the phrase was usually represented by its acrostic O E H B D D E (*O Edel Herz Bedenk Dein End*—"O noble heart consider thy end"). This short expression is the particularly close to the idea of the medieval *Memento Mori*, in that it is frequently directed to readers in the beauty of their youth to think of how death is always at close at hand. The subject of the young man or woman accompanied by a ghastly skeletal image of death was common in murals and sculpture and popularized by "Northern" Renaissance artists such as Albrecht Dürer, Martin Shongauer, and Hans Holbein.

How distressingly young were those to whom this chilling message was so often directed. Embroidered towels were most often—although not exclusively—the work of girls in their teen-age years, perhaps the epitomy of the fair maidens so cruelly juxtaposed with death figures in late-mediaeval paintings and woodcuts. A towel holder from the Landesmuseum in Innsbruck, Austria, is a sculptural statement of this paradoxical image of humanity—so alive and so close to death at one and the same time (fig. 111).

In *fraktur*, the phrase is more commonly written out in full, but occasionally shortened to its acrostic abbreviation. A drawing done by Anna Weber in 1875 places the text within a heart beneath paired birds (fig. 112), while a bookmark done circa 1810 similarly situates the words within a heart from which emerges a flowering tulip (fig. 118) (Weiser, Heaney).

In both New England and Pennsylvania, printed broadsides emphasized the theme of mortality in a widely popular depiction of the Stages of Life, sometimes titled "The Life and Age of Man." By the middle of the nineteenth century printers such as Currier and Ives were publishing and distributing such broadsides to a large public. And even as printed forms were in ready abundance, individual *fraktur* artists continued to make their hand-drawn versions, sometimes adapted from the printed version. An elaborate example shows the progression from cradle to grave, with the moral injunction that the devil will stay away from those who stay away from the devil (fig. 122).

Figure 111: Towel holder. Austria, mid-nineteenth century. Many were the medieval depictions in which youth encounters itself as a skeletal form. The presence of this image on a European towel holder is in keeping with the *O Edel Herz* motif frequently embroidered on towels in German-speaking regions of Pennsylvania. (Courtesy of the Tiroler Volkskunstmuseum, Innsbruck)

A symbolic mode of expression used by numerous *fraktur* artists is that of the flower which fades. In a text of 1807 Schwenkfelder artist Susanna Heebner has written: "I am a blooming flower which soon will fade...." (fig. 109). Her consolation lies in the belief that eternal life resides not in her hope of perpetuated youth, but rather in the new life given by Jesus: "Lord Jesus implant yourself in me, and I will stay standing for ever." Interestingly enough, this lengthy text also contains decorative elements in the form of hearts enclosing the short phrases, "Who knows who soon the walk will end?" and "O noble heart consider your end." Two small presentation *frakturs* illustrated in Weiser (*The Gift is Small*, pp. 116 and 117) feature images of rounded grave-mounds from which issue forth budding flowers, suggestive of heavenly life beyond death. Another kindred text appears on the title page of Maria Lädterman's songbook, with its observation, "As a flower quickly dies, So our life from us flies" (fig. 120). Like the maker of the embroidered towel, the recipient of the illuminated songbook as well as the *Vorschrift* with its chilling declaration of human finitude was very youthful, in many cases not yet ten years of age.

Time/Tempus Fugit

Wie fleucht Dahin der Menschen Zeit
Wie Eilet Man Zur Ewig-keit

How fleeting is human time,
how man hurries to eternity.

Figure 112: Anna Weber. Text and drawing, 1879 (24 cm. x 21 cm., 9.75" x 8.50").

Ontario *fraktur* artist Anna Weber treats the subject of death on several occasions, including this 1879 drawing and text. The circle of hearts is a modification of the traditional *Schädelkreis* (circle of skulls), enclosing descriptions of death as the great leveler of individuals from all ranks and walks of life. (Courtesy of the Canadian Harvest Collection, Joseph Schneider Haus Museum)

This inscription on a bookplate made in 1806 for Gertraut Urffer (fig. 126) has a hymnodic source, taken from the Lobwasser *Vermehrt und Vollständiges Gesang-Buch* printed at Germantown by Christoph Saur (Moyer, p. 216). These must have been chilling words for a young pupil in school in at the beginning of the nineteenth century in Berks County, particularly when accompanied by a winged head similar to those on tombstones of the period.

In that earthly existence is seen to be a period of preparation for spiritual life, the theme of "preparedness" was pervasive in hymnody, devotional literature and also *fraktur*. Many are the religious texts which exhort the believer to prepare for death and the hereafter, with frequent warnings that one can never know when the *Todestunde* will come. The idea of "making every hour" is ubiquitous, expressed with a sense of urgency in a *Vorschrift* made in 1772 by Abraham Heebner: "Before judgment examine yourself... and defer not until death to be justified...." (cf. Moyer, plate 4-34, p. 67).

The theme of time is occasionally given visual expression in Pennsylvania *fraktur* in the form of a "spiritual clock" (*Geistliches Uhrwerk*) which in many cases suggests connections to medieval meditations upon the hours of the day. In some instances, lines of texts make reference to each of twelve hours, frequently outlining traditional symbolic meanings associated with each of the numbers. In other cases, the divisions on the clock face serve as reminders of the gravity of human sinfulness and of the necessity of making atonement every hour of the day. A spiritual wonder-clock of 1798 bears the inscription,

Figure 113: Anonymous. Drawing, early nineteenth century. (12.2 cm. x 8.3 cm., 4.75" x 3.25").
A drawing of eight faces arranged in a circle, probably inspired by the more death-oriented *Schädelkreis* image in Fig. 114. A similar example by this artist is found in the collection of the Free Library of Philadelphia (Weiser/Heaney, Plate No. 151). (Courtesy of the Schwenkfelder Library and Heritage Center)

set within a circle of twelve Roman numerals: "O man, from the depths of your heart, make atonement for every hour" (fig. 127).

A more elaborate *Geistliches Uhrwerk*, is the tall-case clock drawn in 1832 by Andreas Bauer (fig. 128), itself copied from a 1793 example in the collection of the Schwenkfelder Library. Bauer has drawn twelve texts in circles, representing the hours of the day, with commentary on the numerical symbolism of each. Examples include the matter of the number one (only one thing is necessary, that is, to have faith in God), or two (only two ways in which one may care to live), three (the Trinity), etc. The last text has apocalyptic significance, referring to the twelve gates of the new Jerusalem.

An Ontario example, drawn in 1821 by a Mennonite schoolmaster for the pupil Magdalena Albrecht at Vineland, west of Niagara Falls, provides in similar fashion a meditation upon the twelve hours, as well as texts from Pietistic hymnody on the subject of Jesus as lamb and mystical bridegroom (fig. 129). These lines are closely related to mid-sixteenth century stanza, *Der Bräutigam wird bald rufen*, credited to Johann Walter, and set to music a half-century later by Melchior France (in Audemberge's *Christian Worship: Handbook*, and also in Fretz's *Handbook to the Anabaptist Hymnal*, p. 68), extolling believers to shake off their drowsy sleep, to light their lamps, and to be attentive when the Bridegroom calls.

One of the most elaborately detailed versions of the *Geistliches Uhrwerk* is an 1823 specimen attributed to Jacob Merchÿ (fig. 130). The text here reads: "The chimes strike ten; in this hour, show me the Ten Commandments, and the ten thousands pounds which I owe Thee, O righteous God. At ten o'clock, make me pure." The ten thousands pounds is suggestive of the weight of sin and the enormity of the atonement required (beyond the capability of humankind and possible only through divine grace). There is a resemblance in this short commentary to an 1803 Spiritual Clockworks illustrated in Weiser's *Fraktur* (p. 19), which provides a meditation on each of twelve hours. An interesting visual reinforcement to the text in the Merchÿ example is the depiction of the clock face with its hands pointing to the tenth hour.

All of this takes us to the that oft-repeated injunction toward preparedness, expressed at an early date in a 1765 *Vorschrift* by Martin Detweiler, with its caution: "Do not boast of tomorrow's day, for you do not know what will happen today. . . . We do not really know when our course will end. . . . The day and hour is concealed from us. Keep yourself ready for every tomorrow. . . ." (discussed in Yoder's "Fraktur in Mennonite Culture," p. 314).

That these "meditations upon the hours" were intended for reading and reflection seems to be a reasonable conclusion, particularly if we consider the fact that late-eighteenth-century printers brought out versions of the *Haus-Segen*, a *fraktur* form clearly made for display in the Pennsylvania German household. Some of these early printed House Blessings feature decorative enhancements by Henrich Otto and Friedrich Speyer, and contain meditations upon the hours of the day, as the central text expresses the wish that God will bless all those who go out and come in.

With its heavy dose of anxious anticipation of Death's unknown time of arrival, and its prodding of the believer to be in a state of readiness, Pennsylvania *fraktur* also points to the redemptive side of God, and the conviction that the consequence of human sin, i.e., mortality, is in the end overcome by the promise of eternal life and its assurance through divine grace. The concluding lines of the 1803 Spiritual Clockworks are decidedly affirmative on this matter: "I am prepared. O Jesus, bring my soul to the joys of heaven" (Weiser, *Fraktur*, p. 18).

Figure 115: Photograph. Cast-iron stoveplate, late eighteenth century.
This scene derived from medieval woodcuts and engravings presents the figure of Death calling on persons from all ranks and walks of life. No exceptions are offered: *Mensch Sie Müssen Sterben*. (Courtesy of the Mercer Museum of the Bucks County Historical Society)

Figure 114: Ephrata imprint, late eighteenth century.
The medieval *Schädelkreis* became a popular image along with the circulation of *Totentanz* and *Memento Mori* subjects as engraved images. In Pennsylvania, the motif appears in several books printed at the Ephrata Press. (Courtesy of the Lancaster Mennonite Historical Society)

Figure 116: Anonymous. *Vorschrift* for Abraham Oberholtzer, 1782 (21cm. x 32 cm., 8" x 12.75").
The preoccupation with death reaches morbid lows in this *Vorschrift*, with its anguished reflection: "No brief hour goes by that I do not remember that, no matter where I am, Death will put me in the final misery." Made by teachers for preadolescent pupils, such texts must have made gloomy reading for a young audience. (Courtesy of the Spruance Library of the Bucks County Historical Society)

Figure 117: Anonymous. Hymn for Jacob Oberholtzer, 1816 (18 cm. x 15 cm., 7.25" x 5.75"). Not only does the individual have to contemplate his own mortality, but even think upon the grief of his family when he is at the threshold of death: "Alas, my poor wife and child, who weep so bitterly because I am so mortal." The prospect of Death paying a call is so grim that "I break out into a cold sweat." (Courtesy of the Spruance Library of the Bucks County Historical Society)

Figure 118: Anonymous. Presentation *fraktur*, early nineteenth century (12 cm. x 5 cm., 4.5" x 2"). Children were introduced to texts and images of death at a very young age in Pennsylvania German schools, as in this presentation *fraktur* bearing the text *O Edel Herz Bedenk Dein End*. (Courtesy of the Rare Book Department, Free Library of Philadelphia, No. FLP 563)

Figure 119: Anna Weber. Pelicans and text, "O Edel Herz," 1876 (22 cm. x 18 cm., 8.875" x 7.75"). Anna Weber, known to have made several embroidered towels, may well have borrowed the *O Edel Herz* text frequently found on such decorative textiles for her *fraktur* drawing of 1876. (Private Collection)

121

Figure 120: David Kulp. Music book for Maria Lädterman, 1813 (10.5 cm. x 20 cm., 4" x 7.75"). Even the flowers, with their promise of life in the early weeks of spring, serve also to remind the believer that we, like they, must face the inevitable: "As a flower quickly dies, so our life from us flies." (Courtesy of the Winterthur Museum)

Figure 122: Anonymous. Copy of German broadside on Life and Age of Man (31.7 cm. x 39.5 cm., 12.5" x 15.5").
The anonymous artist who copied this German printed broadside, *Das Leben und Alter der Menschen* (the Life and Age of Man) has presented a colorful narrative of life's stages from cradle to grave, advising life's traveler to "avoid the devil" and that "he will flee from you." (Courtesy of the Schwenkfelder Library and Heritage Center)

Figure 121: Anonymous. Drawing and text, 1802. Extending the metaphor of the wilted flower is this reminder of our short time on earth: "Flowers are not always red; we hasten toward death. We cannot remain here, so direct your heart upward." (Private Collection)

Figure 123: Daniel Schumacher. Drawing and text, 1775 (19.7 cm. x 30.1 cm., 7.5" x 12"). *Fraktur* artists treated not only the end of life but occasionally also the end of history. Notable in this regard is Daniel Schumacher's presentation of apocalyptic images in which God will eventually lead the pilgrim to a safe harbor: "God is the helmsman. . . . If it seems stormy today, tomorrow will be still." (Courtesy of the Rare Book Department, Free Library of Philadelphia, No. FLP 697)

123

Figure 124: Daniel Schumacher. Drawing of comet, n.d. (18 cm. x 29.4 cm., 7" x 11.5"). Another apocalyptic vision attracted Daniel Shumacher, namely the 1769 comet seen in the skies over Pennsylvania, inspiring the reflection: "You ask yourselves what this star could mean. If God will punish you, then repent while there is still time." (Courtesy of the Rare Book Department, Free Library of Philadelphia, No. FLP 696)

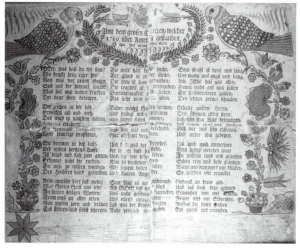

Figure 125: Henrich Otto. Decorations on printed broadside, circa 1785 (32 cm. x 40 cm., 12.75" x 15.625"). The great comet of 1769 inspired another *fraktur* artist, this time Henrich Otto, who made a drawing of it in the form of an eight-pointed star. The text, possibly printed at the Ephrata Press, describes the comet as a sign of divine wrath (*des letzten zornes*) and implores Jesus to help, asking that from this evil sign there may come a good end. (Courtesy of the Ungerbassler Collections of the Phillips Museum of Art, Franklin and Marshall College)

THE URGENCY OF TIME

Figure 126: Anonymous. Bookplate for Gertraut Urffer, 1806 (18 cm. x 11.9 cm., 7" x 4.75").
The theme of time, related to that of mortality, occurs again and again in *fraktur* texts. The words of Gertraut Urffer's bookplate convey an urgent tone: "How fleeting is the human's time, how man hurries to eternity." (Courtesy of the Schwenkfelder Library and Heritage Center)

Figure 127: Attributed to Johannes Moyer. Spiritual wonder-clock, 1798. *Fraktur* drawings of *Geistliche Uhrwerke* (spiritual wonder-clocks) are reminiscent of stylized medieval texts which reflect upon the symbolism of time and the hours of the day. The importance of earthly time, ever so brief, is expressed in the exhortation, "O man, from the depth of your heart, be repentant in every hour." (Private Collection)

Figure 128: Andreas B. Bauer. Spiritual clockwork and text, 1832 (32.3 cm. x 19.7 cm., 12.75" x 7.75"). Andreas Bauer's *Geistliches Uhrwerk* offers a meditation upon the symbolism of the twelve hours of the day. Among its numerical reflections are: *One* thing necessary for salvation (having faith in God), *three* for the Trinity, *four* for the Four Last Things, *five* for the wounds of Christ, *ten* for the number of Virgins who went out to meet the bridegroom, and *twelve* for the twelve gates of the New Jerusalem (Heaven). (Courtesy of the Schwenkfelder Library and Heritage Center)

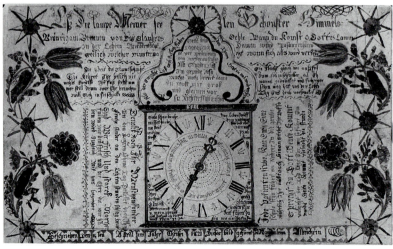

Figure 129: Anonymous. Drawing of clock face and text, 1821. A piece done in the Mennonite community in the Vineland area of Ontario, this text is centered within a stylized clock, with hymn-based words addressing the subject of the soul meeting its heavenly Bridegroom. (Private Collection)

Figure 130: Attributed to Jacob Merchÿ.
Clock and text, 1823.
The brief text is nearly identical to that in the tenth heart in another example, illustrated in Frederick Weiser's 1973 *Fraktur*, p. 19: "The chimes strike ten; this hour directs me to the Ten Commandments and the ten thousand pounds which I would owe Thee, O righteous God, at ten make me pure." To reinforce the point, the artist has drawn the hands on the clock face pointing to ten. (Collection of Bruce Shoemaker)

Figure 131: Anonymous.
Spiritual clockwork and text, 1853.
As in the Andreas Bauer fraktur, this *Geistliches Uhrwerk* comments upon the symbolism of each of the numbers of hours of the day, promising that at the twelfth hour the believer will be united with God. These examples indicate some variety as to symbolic associations. (Collection of Joan Johnson)

Figure 132: Ephrata Cloister music manuscripts. Five-part choral harmony printed at Ephrata, included works by Conrad Beissel and others. Elaborate border decoration done by members of the cloister accompanies text and notation. (Courtesy Ephrata Cloister)

CHAPTER VII

AND THE ANGELS SING:
MUSIC AND FRAKTUR

Singen und spielen

dem Herrn in Euren Herzen

"Sing and make music unto the Lord in your hearts." This brief injunction on the title page of Elisabeth Oberholtzer's songbook of 1803 indicates the importance accorded to musical praise in the German communities of Pennsylvania. In the liturgical traditions of the Lutheran and Reformed communities, music both choral and instrumental was an integral feature of formal worship, reflecting Luther's high esteem for the religious significance of music: "Music is a gift, a benefaction, of God, not a gift of man" (*Tischreden*, No. 7,034). Artist Lewis Miller provided a detailed depiction of Sunday worship in his drawing, "Interior of Old Lutheran Church York, Pa" (fig. 134), in which the choir is positioned around the organ and its enormous bank of pipes in the loft. Something of the importance of the musicians may be intimated by the fact that immediately after the name of the pastor there appear the names of the "Sing Chor" members.

The earliest intrinsic connection between *fraktur* and music among the Pennsylvania Germans is to be seen in the Ephrata Cloisters. Conrad Beissel was committed to gathering, composition, and printing of music from the earliest years at Ephrata. In 1739 his hymnal *Zionitischer Weyrauchs-Hügel* was brought off Christoph Saur's press, dedicated to all "solitary doves that coo in the wilderness." In this same year, Beissel opened a singing school at the Cloister. Beissel might be regarded as one of the earliest American theologians of music in view of his *Apology for Sacred Song* where he writes that the requirement for mastery of song is compliance "with the demand of an angelic and heavenly life" (reprinted in Sachse, *Music of the Ephrata Cloister*, in *German Sectarians* II, p. vi).

From an early date there was intimate association of *fraktur* with music at the Cloister, with an intensive program of illumination of score books, hymnals, and folios, including such notable collections as the *Turtel-Taube* in 1747 and the *Paradiesisches Wunderspiel* in 1754. As in the case of medieval manuscript illumination, visual images do not always exhibit direct correspondences with those of the text whose margins they inhabit. Having said so, it is interesting to note that there is nonetheless a significant degree of correlation between *fraktur* imagery and text in many of the principal Ephrata manuscripts. Guy Tilghman Hollyday has paid particular attention to this matter in his

"The Ephrata Codex: Relationships Between Text and Illustration" (p. 33), arguing that there are important links between hymn texts and *fraktur* images in the margins. Notable motifs which appear in both text and image include trees, the turtledove, and the Crucifixion.

Another intriguing relationship between *fraktur* and music at Ephrata has been examined by Robert Stevenson in his historical overview of American religious music, *Protestant Music in America*. With regard to choral music at Ephrata, Stevenson argues that the connection has to do not only with content but style. The spiritual notion of *Sehnsucht*, discussed previously in the chapter on Pietism, has its literary equivalent in the descriptions of the lonely turtledove cooing in the earthly wilderness, seeking its lover in Heaven. For Stevenson, the connection can also be seen with regard to the matter of style. He argues that there is spiritual intent in Beissel's musical arrangements in which the women's voices perform the principal lines, and the men sing large and awkward intervals. The effect is the evocation of melodic and harmonic tensions that amount in effect to a "musical *Sehnsucht*." Beissel's use of minor keys and augmented chords likewise imbues the music with a sense of unfilled anticipation, echoing the impassioned *Sehnsucht* of the spiritual pilgrim (Stevenson, p. 655).

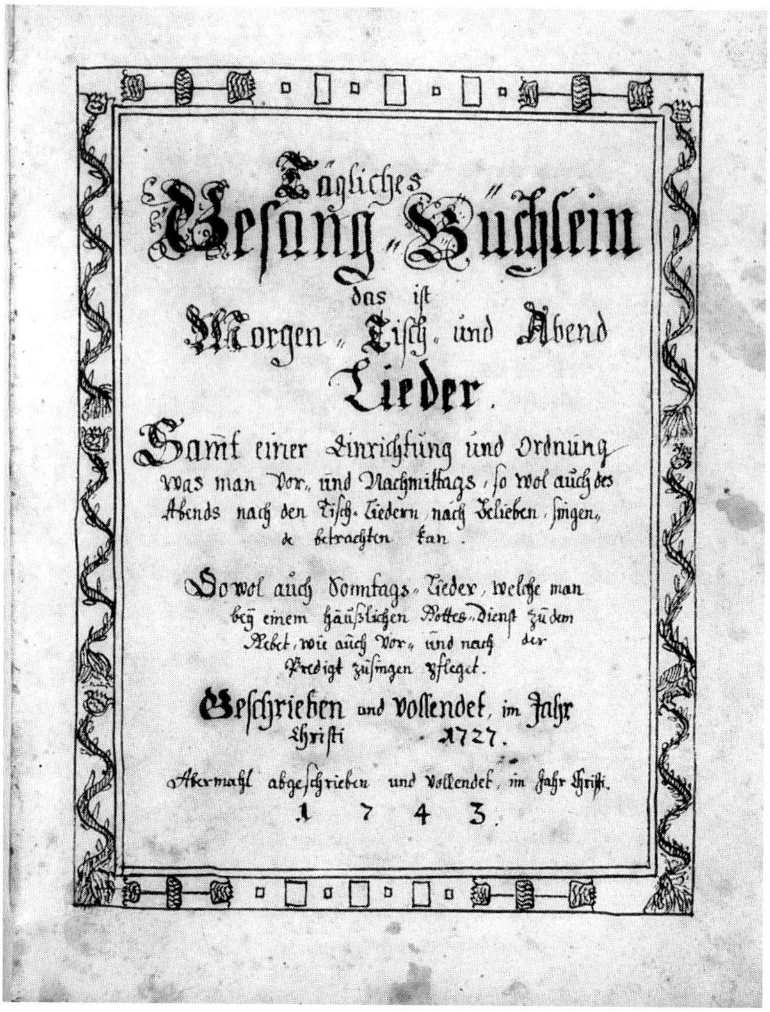

Music was also important in the context of the Pennsylvania German singing school, witnessed by illuminated *Notenbüchlein* made by schoolmaster–*fraktur* scriveners for use by pupils. The singing school may have been a part of the regular curriculum of the Pennsylvania German parochial school, or it may have been conducted separately. It would appear that in many instances the schoolmaster who taught reading, writing, and arithmetic was also the artist who illuminated the title pages of many of the songbooks. The earliest known example of this form dates from 1780, with *fraktur* inscription and drawing attributable to John Adam Eyer. A singing-school booklet inscribed 12 April 1780, made for the pupil Henrich Honsperger, exhorts the young scholar to "Learn by yourself, as you can, to be as a singer, book and a temple...." (cf. Free Library of Philadelphia Collection, FLP B-13). It is the conclusion of Suzanne Gross that Eyer is entitled to be credited with the very introduction of the *Notenbüchlein* into the school curriculum (Gross, *Hymnody*, p. 43).

Fraktur inscriptions on *Notenbüchlein* tend to emphasize proverbs and general rules

Figure 133: Anonymous. Hand-lettered title page, 1743 (19.6 cm. x 15.5 cm., 7.75" x 6").

That music ought to be part of everyday life is suggested on the hand-lettered title page of a 1743 hymnbook, itself copied from a 1727 version. The volume is a "daily hymnbook, containing Morning, Table and Evening hymns.... As well as Sunday hymns which may be used for a household service...." (Courtesy of the Schwenkfelder Library and Heritage Center)

for the moral life. Some are explicit in their references to the virtues of music itself. While all serve the essential purpose of identification of the ownership of the songbook by means of the conventionalized form, *Dieses Noten-Buchlein gehört . . .* or *Dieses Hermonisches Melodeyen Buchlein gehört. . .* , a few examples provide more detailed musical information. A 1788 booklet for Maria Bächtel, attributed to the *fraktur* artist Andreas Kolb, informs us that it contains the "best-known songs from the Marburger Songbook" (cf. Mary Jane Lederach Hershey, "The Notenbüchlein Tradition. . . ," in Amsler [ed.], *Bucks County Fraktur*, p. 123). The interdenominational influences with regard to music and *fraktur* are notable here, with the inscription penned by the Mennonite schoolmaster Andreas Kolb and hymnody used in this largely Mennonite school taken from the enormously popular hymnbook of Pennsylvania Lutherans. The text used by both Kolb and Eyer has been traced by Henry S. Bornemann to the Foreword in the 1765 print of the Marburg Hymnal, and is discussed in Don Yoder's "Fraktur in Mennonite Culture," p. 319):

Willst du in der Stille singen/ Und ein Lied dem Höchsten bringen
Lernen, wie du kannst allein/ Singer, Buch and Tempel sein

Figure 134: Lewis Miller. "Interior of Old Lutheran Church in 1800, York, Pa.," (detail) circa 1820.
This detail of the Lewis Miller drawing of the church interior shown in Fig. 8 emphasizes the importance of music. The text makes specific reference to the choir, whose members and organist are shown making their contribution to the worship life of the "Old Lutheran Lutheran Church" in York. (Courtesy of the York County Heritage Trust)

The popularity of the text is seen by its frequent repetition on the title pages of songbooks over a period of almost three decades, with three examples illustrated in the Weiser/Heaney catalogue *The Pennsylvania German Fraktur of the Free Library of Philadelphia*, all seemingly attributable to artist David Kulp and with dates of 1803, 1803, and 1807 (FLP B-10, FLP B-20, FLP B-1050). The link between *fraktur* and music is an especially close one to the degree that both activities are encouraged as marks of "worth." Indeed, the text regarding music in the 1780 songbook for Henrich Honsperger is accompanied by the observation, "Whoever can do something is highly esteemed. There is no call for an unskilled person," the same words which are attached to references to the

virtue of handwriting in Eyer's 1786 *Vorschrift* booklet for Abraham Hackmann and a similar 1786 example for Abraham Hoch, in the collections of the Schwenkfelder Library and Joseph Schneider Haus Museum, respectively). It would seem that the arts of the hand and the voice alike were regarded as divinely given instruments for work and accomplishment dedicated to God.

Finally, attention may be drawn to elements of continuity regarding the theological subject matter of hymnody and *fraktur* inscriptions. While the content of *fraktur* texts is drawn from a range of sources, scripture, and hymnody assume the greatest importance in this regard. To give but a few examples from the present study, one might cite the following hymnody sources for *fraktur* inscriptions appearing in Moyer's study of *fraktur* in the Schwenkfelder Historical Library collection:

Neu-Vermehrt und Vollständiges Gesang-Buch (Christoph Saur, 1763)

This hymnal of the German Reformed Church was printed in Europe in the sixteenth and seventeenth centuries as well as in Pennsylvania. Among *fraktur* texts in the present volume derived from Ambrosii Lobwasser's hymnal are the following:

Christian Stauffer, Religious Text, 1769 (Moyer, fig. 1-5)
Abraham Heebner, *Vorschrift*, 1772 (Moyer, fig. 4-35)
Diamond-Band artist, *Vorschrift* for Isaac Schultz, 1787 (Moyer, fig. 5-62)
Anon., bookplate for Gertraut Urffer, 1806 (Moyer, fig. 5-63)

Neu-Eingerichtetes Gesang-Buch (Christoph Saur, 1762)

Comprised of hymns collected and composed by George Weiss and Rev. Balzer Hoffman, copied in script in 1760 by *fraktur* artist Christopher Hoffman (1727–1804), this first Schwenkfelder hymnbook was printed by Christoph Saur at Germantown in 1762. *Fraktur* texts taken from this particular hymnal include:

Christopher Hoffman, religious text for Christina Kriebel, 1784 (Moyer, fig. 4-6)
Huppert Cassel, religious text in heart, 1807 (Moyer, fig. 4-20)
Huppert Cassel, text for Susanna Heebner, 1807 (Moyer, fig. 4-21)
Huppert Cassel, lines from text for Susanna Heebner, 1807 (Moyer, fig. 4-22)
Johan Melchior Wiegener, religious text, 1776 (Moyer, fig. 4-23)
Abraham Kriebel, religious text, 1782 (Moyer, fig. 4-24)
Abraham Heebner, *Vorschrift*, 1772 (Moyer, fig. 4-38)
Abraham Heebner, religious text, 1774 (Moyer, fig. 4-39)
Susanna Heebner, text for Abraham Heebner, 1808 (Moyer, fig. 4-46)
Susanna Heebner, lines from text for Maria Heebner, 1808 (fig 4-47) (p. 80) (+scripture) (also from *Das Kleine Davidische . . .*)
Susanna Heebner, text for Susanna Heebner, 1811 (Moyer, fig. 4-48)
Susanna Heebner, text/Golden ABC, 1809 (Moyer, figs. 4-53, 4-54)
Sarah Kriebel, religious text (Moyer, fig. 4-102)
Andreas Anders, text (garden) for Sarah Reinwald, 1787 (Moyer, fig. 4-114)
Balthasar Heydrick, bookplate for Samuel Heydrick, 1813 (Moyer, fig. 4-118)
George Kriebel, text for Matthias Schultz, 1788 (Moyer, fig. 5-5)
Melchior Schultz, *Vorschrift* for Benjamin Schultz, 1781 (Moyer, fig. 5-7)
Melchior Schultz, *Vorschrift*, 1771 (Moyer, fig. 5-8)
Isaac Schultz, music book for Isaac Schultz, 1791 (Moyer, fig. 5-22)

Geistliches Blumengärtlein (Christoph Saur, 1747)

A compilation of hymns by Gerhard Tersteegen, with rhymes, meditations, and other devotional writings, published at Germantown by Christoph Saur in 1747 and again on later dates. Tersteegen, along with Johann Arndt, were authors of the most widelyread devotional books among the Pennsylvania Germans, placing emphasis upon thepietistic themes of intimate personal relationship with God, withdrawal from the world,turning inwards upon oneself and upon the imitation of Christ. The *Blumengärtlein* is a source for the following *fraktur* texts:

Huppert Cassel, religious text (Moyer, fig. 4-25) (p. 56)
Susanna Heebner, labyrinth (Moyer, fig. 4-57) (p. 92)

Das Kleine Davidische Psalterspiel (Christoph Saur, 1744)

Printed by Saur for the German Baptist Brethren at the very early date of 1744, this hymnal is strongly pietistic and was used commonly among Franconia Mennonites and to a degree among Schwenkfelders in the later eighteenth century. Among *fraktur* texts which quote hymn sources in this songbook are:

Huppert Cassel, religious text (Moyer, fig. 1-4)
Christian Cassel, religious text (certain lines and hymns) (Moyer, fig. 1-6)
Huppert [K]assel, religious text for Isaac Heebner, 1767 (Moyer, fig. 4-19)
Huppert Cassel, text for Abraham Heebner, 1773 (Moyer, fig. 4-26)
John Adam Eyer, religious text, 1783 (Moyer, fig. 4-31)
Huppert Cassel, religious text, 1769 (Moyer, fig. 4-36)
Susanna Heebner, lines from text for Maria Heebner, 1808 (Moyer, fig 4-47) (+scripture)
David Heebner, religious text, 1817 (Moyer, fig. 4-61)
Reverend David Kriebel, Vorschrift for Abraham Anders, 1805 (Moyer, fig. 4-81)
Andrew Krauss, birth record for George Krauss, circa 1803 (Moyer, fig. 5-23)
Sun-and-Moon artist, text for Barbara Schultz, 1806 (Moyer, fig. 5-69)
Christina Schultz, religious text (similar to above), 1861 (Moyer, fig. 5-70)

Figures 135 and 136: Hymnbooks popular among the Pennsylvania Germans. Each denominational tradition had its preferred hymn collections and prayer books, some brought from Europe and others printed at various presses in Pennsylvania. The teaching of both music and handwriting was a significant part of education in Pennsylvania German Protestant culture, and the close association of music and *fraktur* frequently took the form of copied or adapted texts. Right: *Das kleine geistliche Harfe der Kinder Zions* **[or** *Zionsharfe***] (1803) (Used by Franconia Mennonites). Left:** *Das unpartheyische Gesang-buch* **(1804) (Used by Lancaster County Mennonites).**

Die Kleine Geistliche Harfe der Kinder Zions (Michael Billmeyer, 1803)

In 1803, Mennonites of the Franconia District published *Die kleine geistliche Harfe* (while a year later the Lancaster group published *Ein Unpartheyisches Gesang-Buch*). These new hymnals of 1803 and 1804 were to replace the older *Ausbund* in Mennonite congregations, although the Amish retained the *Ausbund* and continue to use it to the present day. *Die Kleine Geistliche Harfe der Kinder Zions* is the more eclectic of the two Mennonite hymnals, embracing a range of material from the *Ausbund* to many hymns of later Pietistic leaning. Several *fraktur* texts are derived from this source, including the following:

Maria Heebner, religious text, 1843 (Moyer, fig. 4-66)
Anthony Rehm, BBC for John Petter Hillegass, 1826 (Moyer, fig. 5-75)
Anon., cutwork with religious text for C. K., 1832 (Moyer, fig. 6-7)
Anon., text (list of morals), 1809 (Moyer, fig. 6-40)
G. S., *Vorschrift* for Isaac Bernet, 1822 ("Jesus-friend") (Moyer, fig. 6-55)

Vollständiges Marburger Gesang Buch **(Christopher Saur, Germantown, 1762)**
Among Pennsylvania Lutherans two popular European hymnbooks were the *Halle* Hymnal, originally chosen by Henry Melchior Mühlenberg, and the *Marburger*, which Suzanne Gross has described as "the unofficial hymnal" of Lutherans in America. This volume existed in both Lutheran and Reformed editions (Weiser, "IAE," p. 462). *Fraktur* inscriptions from the "Marburger" include:

John Adam Eyer, text for Angenes Landes, 1783 (Moyer, fig. 4-33)
Andreas Kolb, Songbook for Maria Bächtel, 1788 (Amsler, fig. 88)
Andreas Anders, bookplate for Andreas Anders, 1762 (Moyer, fig. 4-113)

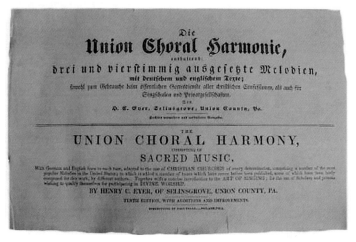

Needless to say, *fraktur* texts are also derived from many other hymn sources, as well, including the Lutheran *Erbauliche Liedersammlung* (1786), the Franconia District's *Zionsharfe* (1803), the Lancaster Conference's *Unpartheyische Gesang-buch* (1804), and the earlier *Ausbund*, the latter of which was used by Rudolph Landes as an inspiration for his extensive *fraktur* text. The connections of this important text in the Philadelphia Free Library Collection (FLP 358) to the *Ausbund*, examined by Don Yoder in "Fraktur in Mennonite Culture," are to be seen both in terms of its acrostic form (used in the *Ausbund* to conceal names of authors of hymns) and its content (sorrowful, mournful tone, reminiscent of *Sterbelieder*).

Perhaps the intimate connections between *fraktur* and music are no better represented than in the life and work of John Adam Eyer, whose career and prolific *fraktur* output have been meticulously researched by Pastor Frederick Weiser. In his definitive study, Pastor Weiser provides many insights into the musical side of Eyer—that he was a pianist and probably also an organist, that he could read and write musical notation, and that he actually owned a copy of C. F. Gellert's *geistliche Oden und Lieder mit Melodien* (containing seven pages of music manuscript in Eyer's hand) (Weiser, "IAE," pp. 460ff.). In addition, his brother John Frederick Eyer was a musician, served as organist of Sharon Evangelical Lutheran Church in Selinsgrove, Snyder County, and published with Isaac Gerhart a *Chorale-Harmonie* in 1818. Frederick's son Henry C. Eyer was a musician as well, publishing in 1833 *The Union Choral Harmony* (Weiser, "IAE," pp. 463–64).

References to music are to be found in numerous Eyer *fraktur* pieces, including title pages of tunebooks and *Vorscrhift* booklets. In addition, it appears that John Adam Eyer can be credited with the introduction of a distinctive form, known as a *Singbild*, a musical text with *fraktur* decoration. An outstanding specimen, in the collection of the Henry Francis duPont Winterthur Museum, was made for Maria Miller in 1789 (fig. 141).

Figure 137: Henry C. Eyer. *The Union Choral Harmony*, 1833. A popular printed choral harmony book, published in at Selinsgrove in Union County. Henry C. Eyer was a nephew of schoolteacher-*fraktur* artist John Adam Eyer. This inexpensive collection of sacred music remained in favor for several decades, going through numerous printings. (Michael Bird Photo)

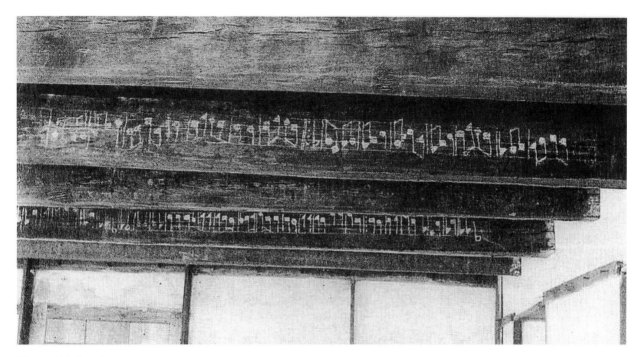

Figure 138: Interior photograph. Deep Run School, Bucks County. It is thought that schoolmaster Samuel Godshalk, who began teaching in 1841, inscribed musical notation on the beams of the Deep Run School in Bucks County in the late nineteenth century, perhaps based on recollections of childhood singing instruction there. (Courtesy of the Spruance Library of the Bucks County Historical Society)

In 1783 Eyer decorated a sheet of a *Vorschrift* booklet (fig. 78) in the most sumptuous detail, with musical images of trumpeting angels accompanying praises of glory ("Holy, Holy, Holy is God the Lord of Sabaoth") and a central framed text which reads:

Du Meine Seele Singe
Wohl auf und Singe schön. . . .

You my soul sing
Arise and sing beautifully

It would seem to be in this same spirit that the *fraktur* artist Johannes Spangenberg (born before 1755–died 1814) drew not only flowers and trees and hearts but also musicians in the margins of his *Taufscheine* and religious texts. Of particular interest in this regard is a large bookplate and text for the pulpit Bible given by the Reverend Michael Schlatter to the Reformed Congregation of Easton. Here a figure plays a trumpet and beside him are lettered the words *Gloria in Excelsis Deo* and *Gott allein die Ehr*, similar to a *Taufschein* done by Spangenberg for Michael Koplin, on which trumpet and horn players are accompanied by the exhortation to give musical praise to God. In his article on Spangenberg, "The Easton Bible Artist Identified," Monroe Fabian suggests that these figures are suggestive of the importance of music, as a special way in which God could be praised. Spangenberg surrounds his musicians with the carefully lettered words:

Singet und preiset Gott den Herrn von ganzen hertzen.
("Let all sing and praise God the Lord with their entire hearts")

Figure 139: David Kulp. Bookplate for songbook for Elizabeth Oberholtzer, 1803 (9.4 cm. x 16.3 cm., 3.5" x 6.25").
The advice on the title page is *Singet und Spielet dem Herrn in Euren Herzen*, "Sing and make a melody unto the Lord." (Courtesy of the Rare Book Department, Free Library of Philadelphia, No. FLP B-10)

Figure 140: Anonymous. Songbook for Magdalena Albrecht, 1834.
Songbooks with notation and decoration by teachers were made widely in Pennsylvania German schools. This example, with its trumpeting angels, was made at the Mennonite school near Vineland, Ontario. (Courtesy of the Jordan Museum of The Twenty)

Figure 141: John Adam Eyer. *Singbild* for Maria Miller, 1789.
In an unusual form specifically titled a *Singbild*, Eyer turns not to scripture or proverb, but rather to hymn texts. As is often the case, references to death are prominent: "My Jesus in my heart, I will not forsake Him.... and when I am finally asked before death, 'Do you have Jesus in your heart?', I will answer, 'yes'." (Courtesy of the Winterthur Museum)

Figure 142: Christina Schultz. Religious text, 1861 (29.2 cm. x 39.7 cm., 11.5" x 15.5"). Direct connections between text and visual image are relatively uncommon. Christina Schultz's religious text of 1861 intersperses drawings of flowers with words from hymnody in *Das Kleine Davidische Psalterspiel*: "Beautifully glitters the glory of the gardens. . . . But how much more beautiful is my lily Jesus Christ." (Courtesy of the Schwenkfelder Library and Heritage Center)

CHAPTER VIII

SYMBOL BY DESIGN:
INTENTIONAL CORRELATIONS
OF TEXT AND IMAGE

My heart consider the good word
and present your work to Christ the King;
My tongue shall be a pen of his holy spirit.
—Christopher Hoffman, 1784

Few Pennsylvania Germans would have been more sensitive to the importance of the written word and its artful expression than the Reverend Christopher Hoffman (1727–1804). He was known in the Schwenkfelder community as a schoolteacher and catechetical instructor—important indications of his religious leadership. Even more significant, perhaps, is his scholarly work as a writer and copyist of early hymn texts. Furthermore, he was an industrious bookbinder, the number of volumes bound by him estimated to have been in the hundreds (Moyer, p. 33). During his eight-year career as schoolteacher in the Skippack School in Montgomery County he made numerous small presentation *frakturs* for his pupils, including this 1784 text for Christina Kriebel (fig. 148). He has borrowed a text from the *Neu-Eingerichtetes Gesang-Buch*, which was printed in 1760 and became the first American Schwenkfelder hymnbook. This book contains hymns composed or compiled by his father and George Weiss and copied by Hoffman himself. In this and several other small *frakturs* made in the 1780s he has succinctly integrated text and visual motif, using a heart frame to focus attention uopn the "*mein Hertz*" text. It is interesting, too, that the text makes reference to the pen, an instrument of special significance to the *fraktur* scrivener.

It is surprising to observe how infrequent are the *fraktur* examples which demonstrate a close connection between text and visual motif. Surprising, perhaps, if one is inclined to take at full value the claim of John Joseph Stoudt that *fraktur* designs are almost inseparable from the literary context; not so surprising if one leans more toward the cautionary view of Frederick Weiser that correlations are comparably rare and that texts themselves are often incomplete or even secular in nature. In "The Ephrata Codex: Relationships Between Text and Illumination," Guy Tilghman Hollyday has examined connections between image and text in Ephrata Cloister manuscripts, a somewhat unique situation as a self-contained spiritual community with its own discipline and capacity for integration of work and life.

Where there is a close relationship between text and image, it is interesting to take note of the motifs which are most commonly found at work. The heart is some ways a most congenial design, because it can also function as a framing device for short texts. Of all examples observed, it is the heart which is most frequently associated with its text, sometimes as the central format of a *fraktur* example such as that done for Christina Kriebel. A most striking example is a bookplate made circa 1800 by Christian Strenge for Barbara Miller (fig. 149), in which a heart serves as the enclosure for the text which begins with a confessional expression, "My heart shall I give to you alone, Lord Jesus," and is followed by an exhortation, "Sing and make music to the Lord in your heart."

In many instances, the heart appears as the central design element in small *frakturs*, whereas in other circumstances it occupies a more marginal position as a border or corner motif on larger religious compositions and *Taufscheine*, frequently enclosing a brief text such as "Give your heart to Jesus." A flower growing out of a heart has a long association with the spiritual notion of good works blossoming from a believing heart.

Flowers and trees are also treated as the subject of texts, even if not as frequently as the ever-popular heart motif. A relatively late *fraktur* composition (1861) for Christina Schultz (fig. 142) is a lengthy text interspersed with large groupings of flowers. The words make references to several kinds of flowers, not necessarily identical to the species pictured—"the sublime lily-flower," "white and red roses," and "all the little flowers." The text has its origins in hymnody, taken from *Das Kleine Davidische Psalterspiel*, and given visual emphasis by the primitive yet bold flowers which appear as the centerpiece of this large composition.

Where flowers abound, birds cannot be far away. Several texts describing the eagle appear in conjunction with this motif, including a noteworthy example illustrated in Frederick Weiser's *The Gift is Small, The Love is Great* (p. 112). The same text is to be found on a printed *Taufschein* (fig. 145) in the Franklin and Marshall College collections.

Figure 143. Abraham Latschaw. Text for Isaac Latschaw, 1822.
An intentional connection of visual image and text is seen in this work done by Abraham Latschaw in the year of his move from Berks County to Waterloo County, Ontario: "Don't the little birds make a commotion as day dawns in the morning; they do not cease their thanks." This text was used repeatedly also by Christian Strenge and an unidentified Lancaster County *fraktur* scrivener working in a style similar to that of Latschaw. (Courtesy of the Canadian Harvest Collection, Joseph Schneider Haus Museum)

Figure 144: Anonymous. Drawing of griffin, with house-blessing text, 1803 (32.6 cm. x 39.5 cm., 12.75" x 15.50").

In addition to the explanatory description of the image ("the griffin is trapped. . . . And can achieve no more thievery in the world"), a most interesting feature of this *fraktur* house blessing is the blunt disclosure of the monetary motivation for its making: "This is a beautiful picture and whoever wants it must pay what it is worth." (Courtesy of the Winterthur Museum)

Another "stock" bird text is used by several artists in and around western Berks and eastern Lancaster Counties, among these Christian Strenge (1757–1828), Abraham Latschaw (1797–1870), and others. Abraham Latschaw's double bookplate for his brother Isaac, executed shortly after their arrival in Waterloo County, Ontario, features two birds flanking the words, "Do not the little birds, making noise with their tongues, give thanks to God at the break of dawn?" (fig. 143). This same text is also used by Strenge in the bookplate previously discussed (fig. 149) in terms of its heart motif. To find a *fraktur* composition with a single correlation of text and visual image is unusual; Strenge's double reference—to the heart and to the birds—is a rarity indeed.

Two more examples are of interest in terms of their heavenly references. Angels are almost ubiquitous decorative motifs on larger *fraktur* specimens, notably *Taufschein* forms, but textual references are seldom found. It is Christian Strenge, once again, who provides a direct connection in decorated title page of a songbook for Maria Schwahr (fig. 146). He has drawn the version of an angel consisting of a winged head on two pages of her songbook. In one case, the angel hovers over a short text which reads: "The angels and the heavens praise and give honor to God; The angels continuously sing and praise God with great acclaim. Halleluja."

The crown appears less frequently than other motifs discussed here, but on occasion its religious significance is made emphatically evident in the words of the text, as in the example discussed by Frederick Weiser at the beginning of his 1973 *Fraktur* volume. The crown appears in this case at the top of a *Taufschein* for Johannes Purmann, a particularly significant context given the theological importance of Baptism as entry into the community and faith and as enabling the believer to anticipate the Crown of Glory in Heaven. Indeed, the text hovering over this visual motif reminds the spiritual pilgrim to "strive for the Crown of Righteousness." A similar integration of word and image is to be found in the case of Abraham Shultz's 1766 bookplate for Barbara Krauss, where the drawing of a crown at the top of the composition is underscored by words taken from 2 Timothy 2:5 at the bottom of the page, indicating that whoever is faithful and stands by the Lord will "get the crown of eternal life" (fig. 147).

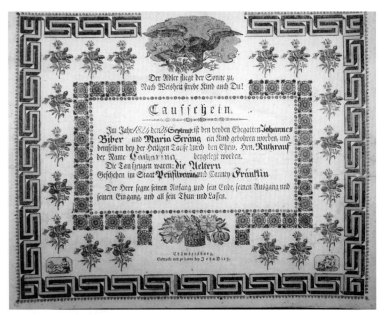

Figure 145: John Dietz. Printed *Taufschein*, circa 1810 (30 cm. x 37 cm., 11.625" x 14.375"). Beneath the eagle on this printed *Taufschein* from Franklin County are the words: "The eagle flies up to the sun, O Child, strive for wisdom." (Courtesy of Special Collections, Franklin and Marshall College)

Whether in other instances *fraktur* artists used visual motifs with deliberate symbolic intent is difficult to establish with certainty, although the case might be reasonably argued with regard to a number of schoolteachers who were personally of strong religious persuasion and were steeped in the diversely religious texts of scripture, prayer, and hymnody. To be sure, in many, if not most cases, aesthetic appeal may have been as central a motivation as the wish to impart religious instruction by visual-symbolic means. In a sea of interpretive uncertainty about motivations generally, it is perhaps a welcome respite to visit the small oasis of *fraktur* in which text and image are sometimes intimately bound together in a meaningful whole.

Figure 146: Christian Strenge. Songbook for Maria Schwahr, 1797 (10 cm. x 17 cm., 3.875" x 6.625"). A broad-winged angel hovers over the words: "The angels and the heavens give praises in honor of God; the angels sing continuously and praise God. . . . Halleluja." (Courtesy of the Landis Valley Museum, Pennsylvania Historical and Musem Commission)

Figure 147: Abraham Schultz. Bookplate for Barbara Krauss, 1766 (33.8 cm. x 21 cm., 13.25" x 8.25").

In this manuscript book copied by Barbara Krauss from a 1586 printed original, Abraham Schultz has drawn a bookplate with juxtaposed crown and biblical verse: "So let us follow the dear Lord with body and soul, and stand by Him in suffering, for whoever does not fight does not get the crown of eternal life" (2 Timothy 2:5). (Courtesy of the Schwenkfelder Library and Heritage Center)

Figure 148: Christopher Hoffman. Text for Christina Kriebel, 1784 (13.8 cm. x 16.5 cm., 5.5" x 6.5").

The heart is frequently utilized as a framing device for texts, in this case with continuity of form and content. The line is taken from hymn 216 in the *Neu-Eingerichtetes Gesang-Buch* of 1762: "My heart consider the good word and present your work to Christ." (Courtesy of the Schwenkfelder Library and Heritage Center)

Figure 149: Christian Strenge. Bookplate for Barbara Miller, circa 1800. An oft-repeated devotional expression, here framed within a heart: "This heart of mine belongs to you alone, O Lord; I give myself entirely to you, Jesus, and sing and make music in your heart." (Private Collection)

Figure 150: Sun-and-moon artist. Religious text for Barbara Schultz, 1806 (27.5 cm. x 34.7 cm., 10.75" x 13.50").
In this elaborately flowered text the artist expresses an almost analogical connection of the world with its divine foundation: "The world has no beauty which does not present to my eyes my most beautiful Jesus Christ, who is the source of beauty." (Courtesy of the Schwenkfelder Library and Heritage Center)

CONCLUSION

THAT WHICH GROWS GREEN
TO THE HONOR OF GOD

Artistic activity is religiously significant because it amounts to the structuring of the world in comprehensible patterns.
—Frederick Streng, *Understanding Religion*, p. 84.

The observation by Streng would seem to admit of few exceptions in the history of human artistic expression—from neolithic cave paintings at Lascaux or Altimira to Persian garden design in the Ottoman Empire or yard art in Kansas. His argument for art's religious significance as a structuring-of-the-world process would perhaps be equally applicable to the that enormous outpouring of hand-lettered texts and drawings of familiar motifs, rendered in conventionalized compositional patterns by schoolmasters and countless other artist-scriveners in rural Pennsylvania.

What could be reasonably added to Streng's analysis is the suggestion that in the phenomenon of Pennsylvania German *fraktur*, the world is not only "structured" in comprehensible patterns," but is in fact already "perceived" as such. The two may in fact be two faces of one phenomenon, since the process of selection already changes the world observed. It may be tempting to say that in traditional folk art, of which Pennsylvania German *fraktur* is an important manifestation, the artist does not seek to change the world, since perpetuation rather than innovation is the dominant motivation in decoration. This observation falls short, however, in its failure to recognize that the inclination to express in a competent hand and through strength of drawn and colored image, the artist engages in beautification, a highly transformative phenomenon which changes the world in no small degree. The ordinarily observed world of nature is rarely as tidy, bright, or orderly as it is in the highly foliated world of Pennsylvania German *fraktur*.

Some *fraktur* compositions are particularly evocative of the divine backdrop of the natural world whose details have caught the attention of scriveners and artists. A religious text attributed to the "Sun-and-Moon artist" makes an intimate connection between nature's array and that of the Lord: "The world has no beauty which does not present to my eyes my most beautiful Jesus Christ, who is the source of all beauty" (fig. 150). One of the most garden-like compositions in *fraktur*, executed in 1787 by Andrew (Andreas)

Figure 151: Andrew Anders. Text for Sarah Reinwald, 1787 (40.7 cm. x 32 cm., 16" x 12.5").
In one of the most beautiful of all *fraktur* compositions, with nature domesticated beyond a garden fence, this text celebrates the beauty of flowers and also the ancient root-of-Jesse metaphor: "I know a little flower pretty and fine.... The branch which carried such came from David.... As Isaiah clearly writes his praises of the little flower, that sprouts as such and is beautifully rooted on a branch of Jesse's stem...." (Courtesy of the Schwenkfelder Library and Heritage Center)

Figure 152: Anonymous. Drawing with text, circa 1800 (17 cm. x 10 cm., 6.5" x 4"). Though there may also be an association with mortality in the ancient belief that a bird carries the soul at death, the religious symbolism of the singing of birds as an offering to the Lord above is also emphasized: "Now see, my child, the flock of birds in Spring when they are singing.... To God an offering bringing...." (Courtesy of the Winterthur Museum)

Anders (fig. 151) is a profusely arranged display of tulips and other flowers behind a picket fence and gate. Its text is symbolic, alluding to the image of Jesse's stem. Perhaps the simple act of looking into the garden will inspire the reflection: "I know a little flower pretty and fine that I like very much. It blooms in God's congregation quite beautiful above all the rest" (translation in Moyer, p. 141). In another example (fig. 152), the singing of ordinary birds constitutes an offering to God. Frederick Weiser does remind us that in some folklore traditions birds were also associated with mortality, carrying away the soul at death. In the present text, immortality seems to have the last word:

So sing, my child, until you are white,
There in heaven's eternal light.

Like the dedicatory inscriptions themselves, *fraktur* texts and drawings sometimes express the view that nature itself is a dedication to its divine source. Maria Heebner's 1853 cutwork valentine (fig. 153) makes use of a familiar phrase: "everything grows green for the honor of God," while a text attributed to Andreas Kolb expresses this sense of celebration in its eloquent lines:

How many pretty little flowers one sees at springtime....
Everything grows green to the honor of God.

Perhaps the epitome of complex detail and elaborate text is the a large composition done by George Geistweite in 1801. Animals of diverse species, birds and human figures, along with the mythological pelican pecking its breast to feed its young—all are gather together in a great profusion of color in association with that great biblical song of praise:

I will praise the Lord at all times. His praise shall continually
be in my mouth. My soul shall make her boast in the Lord,
the humble shall hear thereof and be glad. O Magnify the Lord
with me, and let us exalt His name together.

—Psalm 34:1–3

Of course, *fraktur* art should not and cannot be considered merely as a depiction or even enhancement of nature. It has a thematic focus, or perhaps one should say, a cluster of thematic focal points, so that nature is understood in relationship to implicit religious and moral considerations of the human being's place in the world. Image and text are poles of the central reality of *fraktur* expression, at times intentionally related or otherwise and more commonly bearing implicit connections with one another. To be sure, imagery sometimes become sufficiently detached from earlier textual associations so that it appears to be not so much didactic as decorative in function. But here a cautionary note in favor of the religious argument is in order, since the decorative motifs and their arrangement scarcely differ from those of early *fraktur* compositions. To be sure, the unfolding of the nineteenth century is witness to a changing world, in which text changes to picture, baptismal record to birth record, German language to English, parochial school to public school. Even at the height of *fraktur* production, official church membership and attendance was never particularly high, and evidence that *fraktur* was consciously regarded as religious art by its recipients is not readily available, although enough is known about some artists, particularly schoolteachers, to indicate that some of them were indeed imbued with an impressive degree of religious motivation. To the degree that *fraktur* served both mundane and transcendental purposes, it could not always be so readily reserved for the praise of God alone: *Soli Deo Gloria*. In the recognition, however, that its rewards were both aesthetic and spiritual, it could perhaps be more generally dedicated in most instances simply to the Honor of God, without divine and human dimensions having to exclude one another: *Gott Sei die Ehre*.

In the Protestant world of the Pennsylvania Germans, variously shaped by an already diversified Reformation heritage and frequently transformed by the later dispersion of Pietistic values, certain themes prevailed in *fraktur* texts, as they had been important likewise in prayer and hymn. Prominent among these were the historical understanding of original union with God in Paradise, the radical action of rebellion by humanity's first parents, Adam and Eve, the devastating consequences for later generations manifested in sin and death. Juxtaposed against this image of despair are the many textual meditations on the divine intervention by God through Jesus whose Crucifixion brought Redemption and made possible the anticipation of reconciliation with God in Heaven. One cannot escape the profound, even oppressive, presence of the theme of death in *fraktur* texts, a presence similarly evident in the devotional texts and hymnody of the day. Even in its celebration of the natural world, sometimes perhaps comprehended as the handiwork of the divine hand, *fraktur* imagery seems never far removed from an awareness that its deeper function is to offer chilling reminders, too. Perhaps it was easier to address the subject of life's brevity within the comforting garment of Pietistic spirituality and its tempering of the fact of mortality of the body with the anticipation of immortality of the soul.

The idea of life as a spiritual pilgrimage toward regained unity with the divine is a subject occurring repeatedly in *fraktur* texts, with elaborate variations on the metaphors of the journey, the road and the labyrinth, and the diverse forms of temptation which might lead the knight of faith off the true path to salvation. The emphasis upon death is at times almost overbearing in its grim realism, but even at its bleakest descriptive levels stands in the background of the ever-present themes of mercy, love, and the promise of the crown of glory in that perfect world which shines over the vale of tears below. In text and image, the religious significance of Pennsylvania German *fraktur* may consist precisely in that before-attested function of religious art in general, that it reminds everyone who stand in its presence of one's true home.

Figure 153: Maria Heebner. Cutwork valentine/text, 1853 (31.6 cm., 12.5" diameter). Maria Heebner has copied a 1753 cutwork valentine attributed to Christopher Wagener, but has changed his text about earthly love to one with clearer religious purpose: "Many kinds of decorative flowers come up in gardens and meadows which teach us that everything sprouts for the honor of God." (Courtesy of the Schwenkfelder Library and Heritage Center)

Figure 154: Andreas Kolb. Religious text, 1817 (40.3 cm. x 33.2 cm., 16" x 13").
Rarely is a *fraktur* composition as thorough in its profuse representation of virtually the entire inventory of Pennsylvania German folk art motifs! The text rejoices in the divine purpose of nature's splendid array: "How many pretty little flowers one sees at springtime.... What is taught from this festivity? Answer: Everything grows green to the honor of God." And though flowers wilt, we are reminded to "be of good cheer," because "the bridegroom is near." (Courtesy of the Rare Book Department, Free Library of Philadelphia, No. FLP 714)

If we were to allow *fraktur* itself to have the final word, we could scarcely do better than to turn to one of its smaller manifestations. Simplicity of design and clarity of expression are uniquely concentrated in a beautiful small presentation *fraktur* (fig. 43/156) made by Conrad Gilbert (1734–1812). Its brief text connects earthly and eternal life:

> *Remain pious and be righteous,*
> *for in doing such things*
> *all will lead to a good end.*

Figure 155: George Geistweite. Religious text (Psalm 34), 1801 (32 cm. x 38 cm., 12.50" x 15.125").
Exuberant decoration reinforces the jubilant praise of the sojourner on earth, copied in a meticulous *fraktur* hand by George Geistweite from Psalm 34: "I will praise the Lord at all times. His praise shall continually be in my mouth. My soul shall make her boast in the Lord, the humble shall hear thereof and be glad. O Magnify the Lord with me, and let us exalt His name together." (Courtesy of the Titus G. Geesey Collection, Philadelphia Museum of Art; photography by Lynn Rosenthal)

Figure 43/156: Conrad Gilbert. Presentation *fraktur*, 1787.
Gilbert's exhortation is simple and moderate, reminding us that a life of piety and righteousness will assuredly lead to a good outcome.

BIBLIOGRAPHY

I. Fraktur and Pennsylvania German Folk Art

Adams, E. Bryding. "The Fraktur Artist Henry Young." *Der Reggeboge* (fall 1977): 1–24.

Allentown Art Museum. *Pennsylvania Folk Art.* Exhibition catalogue: October 20–December 1, 1974. Allentown Art Museum, 1974.

Alderfer, Joel D. "David Kulp, His Hand and Pen, Beet [sic] it if You Can: Schoolmaster David Kulp of Deep Run, the *Brown Leaf Artist* Identified." *Mennonite Historians of Eastern Pennsylvania Newsletter* (January 1996): 3–6.

Amsler, Cory M. "Bucks County, Pennsylvania Fraktur." *Antiques* (April 1998): 582–591.

———, ed. *Bucks County Fraktur.* Kutztown: The Pennsylvania German Society, 1999.

Bird, Michael. *Fraktur and Embroidered Towel: The Interconnection of Folk Art Forms.* Exhibition catalogue: October 1–November 30, 1981. Joseph Schneider Haus Museum, 1981.

———. *Germanisches Volkskunst aus Kanada.* Exhibition catalogue: November–December 1984. Alzey, Germany: Alzey Museum, 1984.

———. *Images of Spirituality: Religious Folk Art.* Exhibition catalogue: December 1, 1988–February 21, 1989. Joseph Schneider Haus Museum, 1989.

———. *Ontario Fraktur: A Pennsylvania-German Folk Tradition in Early Canada.* Toronto: M. F. Feheley Publishers, 1977.

———. "Taking It and Leaving It: Mennonite Fraktur in Pennsylvania and Ontario." In *From Pennsylvania to Waterloo: Pennsylvania German Folk Arts in Transition*, edited by Susan Burke and Matthew Hill. Kitchener, Ontario: Joseph Schneider Haus, 1991: 54–65.

Borneman, Henry S. *Pennsylvania German Bookplates.* Philadelphia: Pennsylvania German Society, 1953.

———. *Pennsylvania German Illuminated Manuscripts.* New York: Dover Press, 1964.

Boyer, Walter E. "Adam und Eva im Paradies." *Pennsylvania Dutchman* (fall/winter 1956–57): 14–18.

———. "The Meaning of Human Figures in Pennsylvania Dutch Folk Art." *Pennsylvania Folklife* (fall 1960): 5–23.

———. "The New Year Wish of the Pennsylvania Dutch Broadside." *Pennsylvania Folklife* (fall 1959): 45–49.

———. "Specimens of Sacred Pictorial Poetry." *Lehigh County Historical Society Proceedings* (1944): 44–53.

Breitenbach, Edgar. "*Des Kaysers Abschied* and the First Dance of Death in America." *Der Reggeboge* (January 1978): 4–9.

Brumbaugh, Martin G. *The Life and Works of Christopher Dock: America's Pioneer Writer on Education.* Philadelphia and London: J. B. Lippincott Company, 1903.

Burke, Susan M., and Matthew H. Hill. *From Pennsylvania to Waterloo: Pennsylvania-German Folk Culture in Transition.* Waterloo, Ontario: Wilfrid Laurier University Press, 1991.

Conner, Paul, and Jill Roberts, compilers. *Pennsylvania German Fraktur and Printed Broadsides: A Guide to the Collections of the Library of Congress.* Washington: Library of Congress, 1988.

Dietrich, Richard. *The Dietrich Fraktur Collections.* Chester Springs, Pennsylvania, n.d.

Earnest, Corinne, and Russell D. Earnest. *Papers for Birth Dayes: Guide to the Fraktur Artists and Scriveners.* Albuquerque: Russell D. Earnest Associates, 1989.

Earnest, Corinne, and Klaus Stopp. "Early Fraktur Referring to Birth and Baptism in Pennsylvania: A Taufpatenbrief from Berks County for a Child Born in 1751." *Pennsylvania Folklife* 44, no. 2 (1994/1995): 84–88.

Earnest, Russell, and Corinne Earnest. *Fraktur: Folk Art and Family.* Atglen, Pa.: Schiffer Publishing Company, 1999.

Fabian, Monroe H. "The Easton Bible Artist Identified." *Pennsylvania Folklife* (winter 1972–73): 2–14.

Fraktur: A Selective Guide to the Franklin and Marshall Collection. Lancaster, Pa.: Franklin and Marshall College, 1987.

Friedrich, Gerhard. "The A. H. Cassel Collection at Juniata College." *American-German Review* (August 1941): 18–21.

———. "The Seven Rules of Wisdom." *American-German Review* (December 1944): 15–16.

Garvan, Beatrice B. *The Pennsylvania German Collection.* Philadelphia: Philadelphia Museum of Art, 1982.

Garvan, Beatrice B., and Charles F. Hummel. *The Pennsylvania Germans: A Celebration of Their Arts, 1683–1850.* Philadelphia Museum of Art, 1982.

Gehret, Ellen J. "'O Noble Heart': An Examination of a Motif of Design from Pennsylvania German Embroidered Hand Towels." *Quarterly of the Pennsylvania German Society* (July 1980): 1–14.

Good, E. Reginald. *Anna's Art.* Kitchener, Ontario: Private printing, 1976.

Gross, Suzanne. *Hymnody of Eastern German Mennonite Communities: Notenbuchlein from 1780–1835.* Ann Arbor: UMI Dissertation Services, 1995.

———. "The *Nötenbuchlein* Tradition in Early Franconia Conference Mennonite Communities." *MHEP Newsletter* (Mennonite Historians of Eastern Pennsylvania) (November 1994): 5–8.

Gunnion, Vernon S., and Carroll J. Hopf. *Pennsylvania German Fraktur.* Lancaster: Pennsylvania Farm Museum of Landis Valley, 1967.

Hawes, Lloyd E. "Adam and Eve in the Decorative Arts." *Antiques* (September 1963): 278–282.

Herr, Patricia. *Amish Arts of Lancaster County.* Atglen, Pa.: Schiffer Publishing Ltd., 1998.

Hershey, Mary Jane Lederach. "The *Notenbüchlein* Tradition in Eastern Pennsylvania Mennonite Community Schools, in an Area Known as the Franconia Conference, 1780–1850." In *Bucks County Fraktur*, edited by Cory M. Amsler, 115–149.

Hesse, Clarke. *Mennonite Arts.* Atglen, Pa.: Schiffer Publishing Ltd., 2001.

Hollyday, Guy Tilghman. "The Ephrata Codex: Relationships Between Text and Illustration." *Pennsylvania Folklife* (autumn 1970): 28–43.

———. "The Ephrata Wall-Charts and Their Inscriptions." *Pennsylvania Folklife* (spring 1970): 36–52.

Johnson, David R. "Christian Alsdorff: The 'Earl Township Artist'." *Der Reggeboge* (April 1986): 45–58.

———. *Christian Strenge's Fraktur.* East Petersburg, Pa.: East Petersburg Historical Society, 1995.

———. "Christian Strenge: Fraktur Artist." *Der Reggeboge* (July 1979): 1–24.

———. "The Fraktur of Northeastern Lancaster County." In *From Pennsylvania to Waterloo: Pennsylvania-German Folk Culture in Transitio.* By Susan Burke and Mathew Hill. Waterloo, Ontario: Wilfrid Laurier University Press, 1991: 47–53.

Kapr, Albert. *Fraktur: Form und Geschichte der gebrochene Schriften.* Mainz: Verlag Hermann Schmidt, 1993.

Kaufman, Henry. *Pennsylvania Dutch American Folk Art.* New York: Holme Press, 1946.

Keyser, Alan G. "Gardens and Gardening Among the Pennsylvania Germans." *Pennsylvania Folklife* (summer 1971): 2–8.

Kline, Robert M., and Frederick S. Weiser. "A Fraktur-Fest." *Der Reggeboge* 4, nos. 3 and 4 (September/December 1970): 3–12.

Landis Valley Associates. *Pennsylvania German Fraktur and Color Drawings.* Landis Valley, Pa., 1969.

Lichten, Frances. *Folk Art of Rural Pennsylvania.* New York: Charles Scribner's Sons, 1946.

———. *Fraktur: The Illuminated Manuscripts of the Pennsylvania Dutch.* Philadelphia: The Free Library of Philadelphia, 1958.

Mercer, Henry C. *The Bible in Iron: Picture Stoves and Stoveplates of the Pennsylvania Germans.* Doylestown, Pa.: The Bucks County Historical Society, 1961.

———. "The Survival of the Mediaeval Art of Illuminative Writing among the Pennsylvania Germans." *Proceedings* (American Philosophical Society) 36, no. 156 (1897): 423–432.

Mickey, Robert. "Religious Dimensions of Fraktur." In *Fraktur: A Selective Guide to the Franklin and Marshall Collection.* Lancaster, Pa.: Franklin and Marshall College, 1987.

Moyer, Dennis K. *Fraktur Writings and Folk Art Drawings of the Schwenkfelder Library Collection.* Kutztown: The Pennsylvania German Society, 1997.

Patterson, Nancy-Lou. "Anna Weber (1814–1888): Waterloo County Fraktur Artist." *Mennonite Life* (December 1975): 15–19.

———. *The Language of Paradise: Folk Art from Mennonite and other Anabaptist Community of Ontario.* London, Ontario: London Regional Art Gallery, 1985.

———. *Swiss-German and Dutch-German Mennonite Traditional Arts in the Waterloo Region, Ontario.* Ottawa: Museum of Canadian Civilization, 1979.

Pennsylvania Farm Museum of Landis Valley. *Pennsylvania German Fraktur and Color Drawings.* Lancaster, Pa., 1969.

Pieske, Christa. *Bilder für jedermann: Wandbilddrucke 1840–1940.* Catalogue for exhibition: May 1988–May 1991. Berlin: Museum of German Folk Art, 1988.

———. "The European Origins of Four Pennsylvania German Broadsheet Themes: Adam and Eve; The New Jerusalem—the Broad and Narrow Way; The Unjust Judgment; The Stages of Life." *Der Reggeboge* (winter 1989): 7–32.

———. "Die Memento-mori-Klappbilder." *Philobiblon*, no. 4 (1960): 127–146.

———. "Ueber den Patenbrief." *Beiträge zur deutschen Volks- und Altertumskunde* (Hamburg, Germany) Bd. 2/3 (1958): 85–121.

Robacher, Earl F. "Johan Adam Eyer: 'Lost' Fraktur Writer of Hamilton Square." *Pennsylvania Folklife* (spring 1985): 98–113.

———. *Pennsylvania Dutch Stuff*. Philadelphia: University of Pennsylvania Press, 1944.

Röhrich, Lutz. *Adam und Eva. Das erste Mesnchenpaar in Volkskunst und Dichtung*. Stuttgart: Verlag Müller und Schindler, 1968.

Ruth, John L., and Joel D. Alderfer. "David Kulp, His Hand & Pen: The 'Brown Leaf' Artist Identified?" *Mennonite Historians of Eastern Pennsylvania Newsletter* (January 1995): 4–9.

Seip, Oswell J. "Pennsylvania German Choral Books." *Lehigh County Historical Society Proceedings* (1944): 39–43.

Shaffer, Ellen. "Illuminators, Scribes and Printers: A Glimpse of the Free Library's Pennsylvania Dutch Collection." *Pennsylvania Folklife* (fall 1958): 18–27.

Shelley, Donald A. *The Fraktur-Writings or Illuminated Manuscripts of the Pennsylvania Germans*. Allentown: Pennsylvania German Folklore Society, vol. 23 (1961).

———. "Illuminated Birth Certificates, Regional Examples of an Early American Folk Art." *The New York Historical Society Quarterly* (April 1945): 92–105.

Shoemaker, Alfred L. "Engravings: Adam and Eve Broadsides." *The Pennsylvania Dutchman*, no. 6 (1952): 14–17.

Sommer, Frank H. "German Language Books, Periodicals & Manuscripts." In *Arts of the Pennsylvania Germans*. (A Winterthur Book published for The Henry Francis Du Pont Winterthur Museum.) By Scott T. Swank, et al. New York: W. W. Norton and Company, 1983: 265–304.

Stopp, Klaus. *The Printed Birth and Baptismal Certificates of the German Americans*, vols. 1–6. Allentown, Pa.: 1997.

Stoudt, John Joseph. "The Meaning of Pennsylvania German Art." *The Historical Review of Berks County* (October 1937): 3–8.

———. *Consider the Lilies, How They Grow: An Interpretation of the Symbolism of Pennsylvania German Art*. Pennsylvania German Folklore Society, 1937.

———. *Pennsylvania Folk Art: An Interpretation*. Allentown, Pa.: Schlechter's, 1948 (revised edition of the 1937 volume).

Studer, Gerald C. *Christopher Dock: Colonial Schoolmaster, The Biography and Writings of Christopher Dock*. Scottdale, Pa.: Herald Press, 1967.

Wehmann, Howard H., and Monroe H. Fabian. "Pennsylvania German Fraktur: Folk Art in the National Archives." *Prologue* (The Journal of the National Archives) (fall 1970): 96–97.

Weiser, Frederick S. "Ach wie ist die Welt so toll! The mad, lovable world of Friedrich Krebs." *Der Reggeboge* 22 (1988): 49–88.

———. "Baptismal Certificate and Gravemarker: Pennsylvania German Folk Art at the Beginning and the End of Life." In *Perspectives on American Folk Art*. By Jan M. G. Quimby and Scott T. Swank. New York: W. W. Norton and Co., 1980.

———. "Christian Mertel, the 'C M Artist'." *Reggeboge* (spring 1987): 75–85.

———. "The Concept of Baptism among Colonial Pennsylvania German Lutheran and Reformed People." In *The Lutheran Historical Conference: Essays and Reports* (1970): 1–45.

———. "Daniel Schumacher's Baptismal Register." Allentown, Pa.: The Pennsylvania German Society, 1968: 185–407.

———. "Fraktur." In *Arts of the Pennsylvania Germans*. (A Winterthur Book published for The Henry Francis Du Pont Winterthur Museum.) By Scott T. Swank, et al. New York: W. W. Norton and Company, 1983: 230–264.

———. *Fraktur: Pennsylvania German Folk Art*. Ephrata, Pa., 1973.

———. *The Gift is Small, The Love is Great: Pennsylvania German Small Presentation Frakturs*. York, Pa.: York Graphic Services, Inc., 1994.

———. "His Deeds Followed Him: The Fraktur of John Conrad Gilbert." *Der Reggeboge* (September 1982): 33–45.

———. "IAE SD: The Story of Johann Adam Eyer (1755–1837), Schoolmaster and Fraktur Artist with a Translation of His Roster Book, 1779–1787." *Ebbes fer Alle-Ebber Ebbes fer Dich, Something for Everyone—Something for You*. Breinigsville, Pa.: The Pennsylvania German Society, vol. 14 (1980): 437–506.

———. "Piety and Protocol in Folk Art: Pennsylvania German Fraktur and Baptismal Certificates." *Winterthur Portfolio* 8 (1973): 19–43.

———. "The Place of Fraktur Among the Mennonites: An Introduction to the Fraktur Collection of the Lancaster

Mennonite Historical Society." *Pennsylvania Mennonite Heritage* (January 1981): 2–9.

———. "Samuel Bentz: The 'Mount Pleasant Artist'." *Reggeboge* (April 1986): 33–42.

Weiser, Fredrick S., and Helen Bryding Adams. "Daniel Otto: The 'Flat Tulip' Artist." *Antiques* (September 1986): 504–509.

Weiser, Frederick S., and Howell J. Heaney. *The Pennsylvania German Fraktur of the Free Library of Philadelphia* (2 vols.). Breinigsville, Pa.: The Pennsylvania German Society and The Free Library of Philadelphia, 1976.

Weiser, Frederick S., and Mary Hammond Sullivan. "Decorated Furniture of the Schwaben Creek Valley." *Ebbes fer Alle-Ebber Ebbes fer Dich, Something for Everyone—Something for You.* Breinigsville, Pa.: The Pennsylvania German Society, vol. 14 (1980): 331–394.

Wust, Klaus. *Virginia Fraktur: Penmanship as Folk Art.* Edinburg, Va.: Shenandoah History, 1972.

Yoder, Don. "Christmas Fraktur, Christmas Broadsides." *Pennsylvania Folklife* (December 1964): 2–9.

———. "Fraktur in Mennonite Culture." *The Mennonite Quarterly Review* 48, no. 3 (July 1974): 305–342.

———. "Official Religion versus Folk Religion." *Pennsylvania Folklife* (Winter 1965–66): 36–52.

———. "Pennsylvania Broadsides I." *Pennsylvania Folklife* (winter 1966–67): 11–21.

———. "Pennsylvania Broadsides II." *Pennsylvania Folklife* (spring 1967): 28–33.

———. "The Pennsylvania Germans: A Preliminary Reading List." *Pennsylvania Folklife* (winter 1971–72): 2–17.

———, ed. *The Picture-Bible of Ludwig Denig: A Pennsylvania German Emblem Book.* New York: Hudson Hills Press, 1990.

———. "Religious Patterns of the Dutch Country." *Pennsylvania Folklife* (Special Festival Issue 1960): 2–10.

Yoder, Don, Vernon S. Gunnion, and Carroll J. Hopf. *Pennsylvania German Fraktur and Color Drawings.* Lancaster, Pa.: Landis Valley Associates, 1969.

II. General Religion, Art, and Folk Art

Alexander, Dorothy, and Walter L. Strauss. *The German Single-Leaf Woodcut, 1600–1700: A Pictorial Catalogue* (2 vols.). New York: Abaris Books, 1977.

Andrews, Edward Deming, and Faith Andrews. *Visions of the Heavenly Sphere: A Study in Shaker Religious Art.* Charlottesville: The University Press of Virginia, 1969.

Audemberge, C. T. *Christian Worship: Handbook.* Milwaukee: Northwestern Publishing House, 1996.

Baktiar, Laleh, and Nader Ardalan. *The Sense of Unity: The Sufi Tradition in Persian Architecture.* Chicago: University of Chicago Press, 1973.

Benton, Janetta Rebold. *The Medieval Menagerie: Animals in the Art of the Middle Ages.* New York, 1992.

Berefelt, Gunnar. *A Study on the Winged Angel: The Origin of a Motif.* Stockholm: Almqvist and Wiksell, 1968.

Broderick, Herbert R. "A Note on the Garments of Paradise." *Byzantion* 55 (1985): 250–254.

Brown, Dale W. *Understanding Pietism.* Grantham, Pa.: Brethren in Christ Historical Society, 1995 (revision of 1978 edition).

Butler, John F. *Christianity in Asia and America after A.D. 1500.* Ledien: E. J. Brill, 1979.

Camille, Michael. *Image on the Edge: The Margins of Medieval Art.* London, 1992.

Caviness, Madeline H. "Images of Divine Order and the Third Mode of Seeing," *GESTA* 22, no. 2 (1983): 99–120.

Clark, Willene, and Meradith T. McMunn, eds. *Beasts and Birds of the Middle Ages: The Bestiary and Its Legacy.* Philadelphia: n.p., 1989.

Curley, Michael J. "'Physiologus', and the Rise of Christian Nature Symbolism." *Viator* 2 (1980): 1–10.

DeBreffny, Brian. *The Synagogue.* New York: Macmillan, 1978.

Deetz, James. *In Small Things Forgotten.* New York: Doubleday and Co., 1977.

Dewhurst, C. Kurt, Betty MacDowell, and Marsha MacDowell. *Religious Folk Art in America: Reflections of Faith.* New York: E. P. Dutton, Inc., in association with The Museum of American Folk Art, 1983.

Druce, George C. "The Medieval Bestiaries and Their Influence on Ecclesiastical Decorative Art." *Journal of the British Archaeological Association,* n.s. 25 (1919): 40–82; also in 26 (1920): 35–79.

Eck, Diane. *Darsan: Seeing the Divine Image in India.* Chambersburg, Pa.: Anima Books, 1981.

Eliade, Mircea. *The Myth of the Eternal Return.* Princeton, N.J.: Princeton University Press, 1971 (1954).

Ernst, James E. *Ephrata: A History.* Allentown, Pa.: The Pennsylvania German Folklore Society, 1963.

Field, Mike. *Symmetry in Chaos: A Search for Pattern in Mathematics, Art and Nature.* Oxford: Oxford University Press, 1992.

Ford, Alice. *Edward Hicks: Painter of the Peaceable Kingdom.* New York: Abbeville Press, 1985.

Fretz, Clarence Y. *Handbook to the Anabaptist Hymnal.* Hagerstown, Md.: Deutsche Buchhandlung, 1989.

Graham, Victor E. "The Pelican as Image and Symbol." *Revue de littérature comparée* 36 (1962): 235–243.

Harper, J. Russell. *A People's Art: Primitive, Naïve, Provincial and Folk Painting in Canada.* Toronto: McClellan and Stewart, 1974.

Hassig, Debra. *Medieval Bestiaries: Text, Image, Ideology.* Cambridge: Cambridge University Press, 1995.

Jobe, Joseph. *Ecce Homo.* New York: Harper and Row Publishers, 1962.

Klingender, F. *Animals in Art and Thought to the End of the Middle Ages.* London, 1971.

Krimmel, Bernd. *Symmetrie in Kunst, Natur und Wissenschaft.* Darmstadt: Mathildenhohe, 1986.

Luther, Martin. *Tischreden.* Wien: Herder, 1983.

McColloch, Florence. *Mediaeval Latin and French Bestiaries.* Chapel Hill: The University of North Carolina Press, 1960.

Miles, Margaret. *Image as Insight: Visual Understanding in Western Christianity and Secular Culture.* Boston: Beacon Press, 1985.

Praz, Mario. *Studies in Seventeenth-Century Imagery.* Roma: Edizioni di storia e letteratura, 1964.

Purce, Jill. *The Mystic Spiral.* London: Thames and Hudson, 1974.

Randall, Lilian M. *Images in the Margins of Gothic Manuscripts.* Berkeley: University of California Press, 1966.

Read, Herbert. *The Origins of Forms in Art.* New York: Horizon Press, 1965.

Reichmann, Felix, and Eugene E. Doll. *Ephrata As Seen by Contemporaries.* Allentown: The Pennsylvania German Folklore Society, 1952.

Roth, Cecil, ed. *Jewish Art: An Illustrated History.* New York: McGraw-Hill, 1961.

Sachse, Julius Friedrich. *The German Sectarians of Pennsylvania 1708–1800.* New York: AMS Press, 1971 (reprint of 1899–1900 volumes).

———. *Music of the Ephrata Cloister; also Conrad Beissel's treatise on music as set forth in a preface to the "Turteltaube" of 1747, amplified with facsimile reproduction of parts of the text and some original Ephrata music of the Weyrauchs Hügel, 1739, etc.* New York: AMS Press, 1971.

Steele, Thomas J. *Santos and Saints.* Santa Fe: Ancient City Press, 1974.

Stevenson, Robert. *Protestant Music in America.* New York: W. W. Norton and Company, 1966.

Stoeffler, F. Ernest. *Continental Pietism and Early American Christianity.* Grand Rapids, Mich.: William B. Eerdmans Publishing Company, 1976.

———. "Mysticism in the German Devotional Literature of Colonial Pennsylvania." *Pennsylvania German Folklore Society* 14 (Allentown, 1950): 1–171.

Stoltzfuss, Isaac. *Hymn Translations [German to English] from* Ausbund *and* Liederbuch. Aylmer, Ontario: Private Printing, 1998.

Streng, Frederick. *Understanding Religious Man.* Encino, Calif.: Dickenson Publishing Company, 1969.

Vlach, Michal, and Simon J. Bronner. *Folk Art and Art Worlds.* Ann Arbor: University of Michigan Research Press, 1986.

Wroth, William. *Images of Penance, Images of Mercy.* Norman: University of Oklahoma Press, 1991.

Yapp, Brundson. *Birds in Medieval Manuscripts.* New York, 1981.

INDEX

A
Adam and Eve, 18, 50, 62, 63, 64, 65, 66, 67, 68, 69, 70, 71, 72, 73, 78, 80, 148
Adams, E. Bryding, 29
Albrecht, Magalena, 119, 136
Ambrose of Milan, 94
Amish, 11, 12, 19, 26
Anabaptists, 10, 19, 26, 86, 89
Anders, Abraham, 133
Anders, Andrew (Andreas), 132, 134, 145, 146, 147
Anders, George, 104
Andrews, Edward, 17
Andrews, Faith, 17
angels, 40, 63, 141
Anglo-American folk art, 18
Apostles' Creed, 25, 45
architectural subjects, 27
Aristotle, 12
Armbrust, Johannes, 78, 80
Arndt, Johann, 52, 54, 90, 95, 97, 107, 133
art and religion, 10, 11, 12, 13, 14
Augustine, 85

B
Bachman, John, 27, 37
Bächtel, Maria, 131, 134
Bähr, Johannes, 44
baptism, 10, 20, 23, 26, 27, 28, 29, 30, 31, 32, 33, 142
baptismal certificates, 19
Bard, Johannes, 27
Bauer, Andreas, 97, 119, 126, 127
Bauman, J. (Ephrata), 64, 73
Bauman, Joseph D., 64, 67, 73
Bedenk Dein End, 117
Beissel, Conrad, 11, 22, 24, 90, 95, 128, 129, 130
believer's baptism, 10, 19, 26, 27
Bentz, Samuel, 27, 38
Bentzinger, Daniel, 29, 34
Bergman, Ingmar, 116
Berks County artist, 33
Bernard of Clairvaux, 90
Bernet, Isaac, 134
birds, 13, 15, 36, 43, 63, 141, 147
birth-and-baptismal certificates, 14, 19, 22, 26, 27, 28, 29, 30, 32, 33, 35, 44, 63, 67, 74, 103
birth-only records, 18, 20, 27, 37, 38, 69, 100
Bixler, David, 45
Bloesch, Donald, 59
Boehme, Jacob, 24, 52
bookplates, 16, 17, 23, 58, 99, 125, 136, 143

Bornemann, Henry S., 131
Brethren, 26
Brubacher, Hans Jacob, 44, 46, 58, 59
Bruckman, C. A., 64
Buddhism, 11
Burkholder, Anna Maria, 36
Busskampf (struggle with sin), 54
Byzantine icons, 9, 40
Byzantine images, 39, 40

C
Cassel, Christian, 133
Cassel, Huppert, 25, 59, 61, 86, 95, 132, 133
Cassel, Joel, 98, 99
Chartres Cathedral, 109
Chosen, The, 11
Church community, 23, 26
Church theology, 10
Church type, 11, 26, 27, 36
Clemer, Maria, 89, 98
clergy *fraktur* artists, 29
comet, 124
confirmation certificate, 103
crown, 142
Crucifixion of Jesus, 14, 50, 63, 78, 79, 80, 81, 82, 83, 94, 107, 111, 130
Currier and Ives, 117

D
Dance of Death, 115, 116
Das Kleine Davidische Psalterspiel, 133
death record, 104. 116
death theme, 10
deBreffny, Brian, 29
Deep Run Schoolhouse, 41, 135
Deetz, James, 18
Denig, Ludwig, 63, 80, 95
Denlinger, Anna, 99
Denlinger, Johannes, 99
Des Kaysers Abschied, 115, 116
Detweiler, Martin, 119
Die Kleine Geistliche Harfe der Kinder Zions, 133
Diefenbach, Daniel, 103
Dietz, John, 142
disdain for world, 56
Dock, Christopher, 41
Dornbach, Anna Maria, 33
Dulheuer, Henrich Otto, 32, 35, 36
Dürer, Albrecht, 64, 67, 109, 117
Dutye, Henry, 34

E
eagles, 140, 142
Ebersol, Barbara, 23

Eby, Amanda, 115
Egelmann, C. F., 78
Ehre seÿ gottin der höhe (Honor to God in the Highest), 149, 151
Ehre Vater artist, 58, 60
El Greco, 95
Eliade, Mircea, 13
embroidered samplers, 18
embroidered towels, 116, 121
Enck, Augustus, 28, 33
Ephrata Cloister *fraktur*, 63
Ephrata Cloister Press, 22, 32, 35, 116, 120
Ephrata Cloister, 11, 18, 19, 20, 22, 24, 32, 54, 63, 90, 91, 94, 95, 105, 115, 128, 129, 139
ex-votos, 14, 17
Eyer, Henry C., 134
Eyer, John Adam, 15, 21, 40, 54, 58, 59, 60, 61, 84, 86, 90, 130, 131, 132, 133, 134, 135, 136
Eyer, John Frederick, 134

F
Faber, Wilhelm Antonius, 28, 33
Fabian, Monroe, 135
family record, 18, 102
first parents (Adam and Eve), 67, 148
fraktur decoration, 13, 14, 19, 20
fraktur images, 9, 39
fraktur text and drawing, 118, 121, 123
fraktur texts, 10, 13, 19, 20, 21, 42, 45, 54, 58, 59, 63, 72, 74, 93, 95, 98, 106, 114, 124
France, Melchior, 119
Francke, August Hermann, 54
French Canadian folk art, 14, 17

G
gardens, 63, 140, 144, 145, 146, 149
Geistlicher Irrgarten, 109
Geistliches Blumengärtlein, 132
Geistliches Uhrwerk (spiritual wonder-clock), 118, 119, 125, 126
Geistweite, George, 147, 150
Gellert, C. F., 134
Gerhard, Anna Maria, 2
Gerhart, Isaac, 134
German Protestantism, 9, 14, 19
Gilbert, Conrad, 2, 151
Giotto, 74
Glätz, Lydia, 27, 38
Godshalk, Samuel, 135
Golden ABC, 51
Golgotha, 69, 109
Gott Sei die Ehre, 148
Gott Sei Ehre, 10

Gottschall, Martin, 64, 69
griffin, 141
Gross, Maria, 58, 60
Gross, Suzanne, 86, 130, 134
Grov, Johannes, 37

H

Hackmann, Abraham, 132
Haus-Segan, 47
Haverstick, Eli, 27, 37
heart religion, 12, 58, 59
hearts, 13, 16, 36, 47, 59, 60, 61, 136, 137, 140, 141, 143, 148
Heebner, Abraham, 25, 42, 65, 133
Heebner, David, 133
Heebner, Isaac, 86, 95, 133
Heebner, Maria, 55, 56, 58, 65, 132, 133, 134, 147, 148
Heebner, Susanna, 25, 48, 88, 91, 105, 107, 108, 109, 110, 114, 132, 133
Hereford Township artist, 89, 92
Herr, David, 23
Hesse, Herman, 11
Heydrick, Balthasar, 132
Heydrick, Samuel, 132
Hicks, Edward, 18
Hillegass, John Petter, 134
Himmelsfahrt (Heavenly Journey), 105
Hinduism, 11
Hoch, Abraham, 132
Hoevelmann, Arnold, 97
Hoffman, Balzer, 132
Hoffman, Christopher, 132, 139, 143
Holbein the Younger, Hans, 115, 117
Hollyday, Guy Tilghman, 129, 139
Holy Family, 17, 63
homelessness theme, 58
Honsperger, Henrich, 130, 131
Hoover, Christian L., 27, 29, 36
Hoover, Daniel, 36
Horst, David, 102
Horst, Magdalena (Martin), 102
Hunsicker, Issac Z., 2, 43, 47, 49, 102
Hutterian Brethren, 26
hymns, 10, 19, 21, 22, 24, 54, 56, 57, 59, 121
hymnbooks, 25, 54, 59, 88, 130, 133, 134

I

illuminated prayer book, 39
illuminations, 24
imago dei, 21
institutional settings, 23
inwardness (Pietism), 56
Irenaeus, 85
Irrgarten (garden maze), 108, 109, 110
Islam, 11, 12

J

Jesus as "sweet Jesus," 58, 86
Jesus as a flower, 93, 94
Jesus as a Good Shepherd, 78, 93, 94

Jesus as friend, 54, 85, 86, 89, 95
Jesus as Lamb of God, 90, 119
Jesus as Light to the World, 89
Jesus as mystical bridegroom, 84, 85, 90, 119
Jesus as pelican feeding its young, 85, 88, 91, 92, 94
Jesus as Second Adam, 24, 85, 89, 99
Jesus as teacher, 85, 89, 96, 98
Jesus as the Man of Sorrows, 95
Jesus as the Suffering Christ (wounded), 17, 85, 94, 95, 97, 98, 99
Jesus as turtledove, 85, 87, 88, 91
Jesus in *Ecce Homo*, 95
Jesus in *Physiologus*, 91, 94
John of Damascus, 10
Judaism, 11, 12, 29

K

Kiess, Johannes, 82
Kobel, Friederich, 104
Kolb, Andreas, 21, 25, 34, 131, 134, 147, 149
Koplin, Michael, 135
Krauss, Andrew, 133
Krauss, Barbara, 142, 143
Krauss, George, 133
Krauss, Regina, 51
Krebs, Friedrich, 63, 70, 72, 74, 76, 79, 80, 82, 83
Kriebel, Abraham, 56, 57, 132
Kriebel, Christina, 139, 140, 143
Kriebel, David, 60, 93, 94, 133
Kriebel, George, 132
Kriebel, Sarah, 132
Kulp, David, 122, 131, 136

L

labyrinths, 105, 106, 107, 108, 109
Lädterman, Maria, 118, 122
Landes, Angenes, 54, 134
Landes, Rudolph, 134
Latschaw, Abraham, 140, 141
Latschaw, Isaac, 140
Laval, Bishop, 14
Lepper, Wilhelm, 36
Life and Age of Man, 117, 122
Linnaeus, Carolus, 12
Liscov, Salomo, 117
Lobwasser, Ambrosii, 9, 132
Lochbaum, Joseph, 27, 36
Lord's Prayer, 44, 111
Luther, Martin, 129
Lutheran Church, 11, 19, 20, 22, 23, 25, 26, 29, 45, 54, 59, 61, 89, 90, 97, 129, 131, 134

M

Manger, George, 73
Marburger songbook, 131
Marquand, Maria, 82
marriage record, 34, 70, 75, 103
Martin, Elizabeth, 116

Marty, Martin, 59
May, D., 78, 80
Mäyer, Catharina, 67
mazes, 108, 110
meditations upon hours, 119, 120
Memento Mori, 115, 116, 117, 120
Mennonites, 11, 12, 19, 20, 23, 25, 26, 27, 29, 30, 35, 36, 54, 58, 59, 86, 90, 95, 97, 119, 126, 131, 133, 136
Mercer, Henry C., 64, 116
Merchÿ, Jacob, 127
metamorphic puzzle, 50
Meyer, Barbara, 42
Meyer, Jacob, 15
Mickey, Robert, 20
Miles, Margaret, 9, 12
Miller, Barbara, 140, 143
Miller, Lewis, 28, 80, 129, 131
Miller, Maria, 134, 136, 137
Miller, Valentin, 35
Montelius, Peter, 104
Moravians, 11, 19, 54, 59
mortality and immortality, 148
mortality, 10
Moser, Daniel, 103
Moses, 11
Moyer, Dennis, 20, 25
Moyer, Johannes, 106, 125
Muhammed, 11
Mühlenberg, Henry Melchior, 134
multipurpose documents, 44
music books, 58, 122
My Name is Asher Lev, 11
mystical bridegroom, 24, 84

N

naming of child, 23, 26
Nativity, 63
needlework, 10
Neu-Eingerichtetes Gesang-Buch, 132
Neu-Vermehrt und Vollständiges Gesang-Buch, 132
New Year's greetings, 46, 59
Noah's ark, 102
Notenbüchlein, 21, 130

O

O Noble Heart Consider Thy End, 10
Oberholtzer, Abraham, 116, 120
Oberholtzer, Elizabeth, 129, 136
Oberholtzer, Jacob, 121
OEHBDDE, 117
Otto, Henrich, 64, 94, 109, 110, 124
Otto, Johann Henrich, 32

P

pacifist outlook, 10
painted chest, 62
palindrome, 110, 111, 112
parochial school, 25
Peaceable Kingdom, The, 18
pelican feeding its young, 92, 147
pelicans, 121

Penn, William, 18, 19
Pennsylvania German folk art, 9, 11, 12, 13, 19, 20, 21, 25, 27, 63, 78, 83, 84, 85, 86, 90, 91, 107, 116, 139, 145, 149
pictorial *fraktur*, 63
Pieske, Christa, 20
Pietism, 9, 10, 12, 18, 20, 25, 52, 53, 54, 55, 56, 57, 58, 59, 61, 86, 87, 89, 95, 106, 107, 119, 130, 134, 148
pilgrimage, 109
plain community, 11, 23, 25, 26, 27
plain people, 12, 17, 18, 19, 26, 27
plain style, 18
Potok, Chaim, 11
Potzer, Maria, 28
presentation *frakturs*, 2, 8, 13, 19, 41, 43, 58, 60, 92, 98, 121, 149, 151
primers, 18
Prodigal Son, 64, 74, 75, 76, 77, 78, 80
Puritans, 18
Purmann, Johannes, 142
Putzer, Maria, 28
Puwelle, Arnold, 63, 79, 80, 107
puzzle (Durs Rudy), 110

Q
Quakers, 18, 19

R
Rausch, Johan Henrich, 29
redemption, 10
Reformed Church, 8, 11, 19, 20, 22, 23, 25, 26, 45, 54, 59, 129, 132, 134
Rehm, Anthony, 134
Reinwald, Sarah, 132, 146
religare, 11
religio, 11, 12
religion, 11
religion and art, 10, 11, 12, 13, 14
religious art, 11, 12
religious folk art, 14
religious text, 55, 57, 61, 105, 138, 149, 150
Resurrection, 24
Roman Catholic *fraktur*, 14, 17, 39, 79, 83
Roth, Cecil, 12
Royer, David, 100
Rudy, Durs, 31, 50, 63, 64, 71, 74, 75, 79, 80, 81, 83, 89, 96, 110

S
Sage, Heinrich, 64
Salvation, 111
Saul, 11
Saur, Christop, 109, 118, 129, 132, 133
Schädelkreis (circle of skulls), 115, 116, 119
Schäfer, Philip, 83

Schlatter, Michael, 8, 135
Schmidt, Catharine, 70
schoolmasters as *fraktur* practitioners, 28, 29, 41, 43, 44, 54, 61, 74, 95
Schultz, Abraham, 16, 17, 142, 143
Schultz, Andreas, 58
Schultz, Barbara, 133, 144
Schultz, Benjamin, 132
Schultz, Christina, 133, 138, 140
Schultz, Isaac, 132
Schultz, Matthias, 132
Schultz, Melchior, 132
Schumacher, Daniel, 28, 29, 34, 103, 123, 124
Schwahr, Maria, 142
Schwenkfelder *fraktur*, 11, 16, 17, 19, 23, 25, 26, 48, 58, 59
sectarian theology, 10
Sehnsucht (spiritual longing), 54, 59, 130
Seven Rules of Wisdom, 48
Seventh Seal, 116
Shaker arts, 18
Shongauer, Martin, 117
Siddhartha, 11
sin and salvation, 148
sin, 10
Singbild, 134, 136
Soli Deo Gloria, 10, 15, 148
songbooks, 10, 40, 60, 136, 142
Spangenberg, Johannes, 8, 28, 112, 135
Spanish American folk art, 17
Spener, Philipp Jakob, 54, 56
Spengler, Maria Magdalena, 103
Speyer, Friedrich, 67, 69
spirit drawings, 18
spiritual wonder-clock, 118, 119, 125, 126
St. Bridget of Sweden, 95
St. Francis of Assisi, 95
St. John Chrysostrom, 90
stages of life, 102
Stauffer, Maria, 79
Steltz, Christian, 70
Stevenson, Robert, 130
Stoeffler, F. Ernest, 26, 107
Stopp, Klaus, 80, 83
Stoudt, John Joseph, 13, 20, 90, 139
stoveplates, 64, 67, 116, 120
Strausbaugh, Sarah, 38
Streng, Frederick, 13, 145
Strenge, Christian, 13, 140, 141, 142, 143
Sun-and-Moon artist, 133, 144
Sussel-Washington artist, 28
Sweet Jesus, 58, 86

T
Taufschein (baptismal record), 20, 22, 23, 25, 26, 27, 28, 29, 30, 33, 34, 36, 37, 40, 44, 67, 69, 73, 83, 102, 103, 140, 142
Tauler, Johan, 107, 109, 110
Tersteegen, Gerhard, 52, 54, 132, 133

textile arts, 19
title page, 130
tombstones, 18, 19, 116
Totentanz (Dance of Death), 115, 116
towel-holder, 117
Tree of Knowledge, 67, 69
Trinity, 45
Troeltsch, Ernst, 26, 27
Turtel-Taube (turtle-dove), 24, 80, 91, 94, 129
turtledove (as songbird), 24, 130
two ways theme, 106

U
Union Choral Harmony, 134
Urffer, Gertraut, 118, 125
Ur-Source, 13

V
via cruces, 109
Vollständiges Marburger Gesang-Buch, 134
Vom Wahren Christentum, 54
Vorschrift (writing exercise) 19, 20, 23, 25, 26, 29, 42, 43, 44, 87, 89, 91, 92, 93, 94, 98, 99, 116, 118, 119, 120, 132, 134

W
Wagener, Christopher, 148
Walter, Johann, 119
Walther, Johan, 90
Weber, Anna, 23, 56, 58, 94, 115, 116, 117, 118, 121
wedding wish, 35
Weinmann, Maria, 29, 34
Weiser, Frederick S., 9, 13, 20, 21, 26, 27, 28, 29, 37, 58, 115, 127, 134, 139, 140, 142, 147
Weiss, George, 132, 139
West, Benjamin, 18
Westall, Richard, 18
Weydmann, Jacob, 32
Wiedergeburt (rebirth), 54
Wiegener, Johan Melchior, 132
Wild, Georg, 34
Wundar Spiel, 24

Y
yard artists, 13
Yoder, Don, 19, 20, 26, 63, 80, 95, 97, 107, 116, 117, 131, 134
Young, Henry, 29, 63, 80, 82

Z
Zinck, John, 100
Zinzendorff, Nikolaus von, 95
Zionitischer Weyrauchs Hügel, 80

ABOUT THE AUTHOR

Michael Bird is a Professor of Religious Studies at the University of Waterloo, with teaching and research interests in the area of religion, cinema, art and folk art. He has organized exhibitions in the United States, Canada, England, and Germany as well as conferences on religion and artistic expression. Among his publications or edited volumes are *Religion in Film* (University of Tennessee Press, 1982), *Ontario Fraktur* (M. F. Feheley Publications, 1977), *Canadian Folk Art* (Oxford University Press, 1983), *Religion, Art and Interreligious Dialogue* (University Press of America, 1994), *Canadian Country Furniture 1675–1950* (Stoddart, 1994), and *Spiritual Journeys in the Films of Ingmar Bergman* (Edwin Mellen Press, forthcoming 2003). With his wife, Susan Hyde, he is co-author of *Hallowed Timbers: Wooden Churches of Cape Breton* (Boston Mills Press, 1994). He is also a contributor to numerous recent volumes including *Anno Domini: Images of Jesus in Art* (Alberta Provincial Museum, 2001) and to *Bucks County Fraktur* (Cory Amsler, Editor: The Pennsylvania German Society, 2000).